The Virgin
Mary
IN THE LIGHT
OF THE
WORD OF GOD

Praise for *The Virgin Mary*

*R*EADERS of books about Mary, the blessed mother of Jesus, have seen much that confuses, but here is a relevant study that clarifies her role and significance.

This book by Dr. Mikhail and Dr. Farag is to be read alongside F. J. Moloney's *Mary, Woman and Mother* and Jaroslav Pelikan's *Mary Through the Centuries*. I highly recommend this work as a balanced and Biblical portrait.   Dr. James Massey
Dean Emeritus of Anderson University School of Theology
"One of the 25 most influential preachers of the past 50 years." – *Christianity Today*

*I*N this outstanding book, the author Dr. Mikhail and his contributor Dr. Farag have examined the intercessary functions, miracles, and titles ascribed to blessed Mary the mother of Jesus, and they set forth a brilliant defense and description from Scripture of the ministries of the Lord Jesus Christ.

For all who work in the Muslim world, this book is a must-read. It clarifies misunderstandings about the triune God—Father, Son, and Spirit—while giving due and proper honor to Mary.

Dr. Don McCurry
Author, and worldwide speaker; active in international missionary training programs in Colorado and Spain.
Former Professor, Fuller Theological Seminary

*W*ITH so few informative books focused on the mother of our Lord, it is encouraging that leading Christian scholars have put in countless hours to reveal the true Biblical perspective.

Sister Ruth Brewer
San Diego, California

*W*E warmly welcome this book, which applies the searchlight of the Bible to the facts about the role of Mary. Today's seekers and believers will benefit from the clear presentation in this excellent book.   Dr. Bill Jackson
Borden, Indiana

*U*SING the sword of the Spirit and the balm of the Gospel, Dr. Mikhail and Dr. Farag illuminate Mary and present deep Biblical concepts with clarity in easy-to-read English.

Rev. Neil Cullan McKinlay
Presbyterian Church of Australia and Army Chaplain
Queensland, Australia

The Virgin

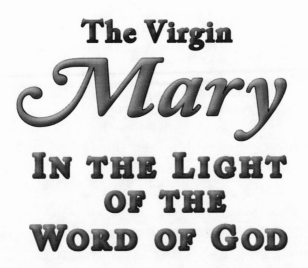

Mary

IN THE LIGHT OF THE WORD OF GOD

DR. LABIB MIKHAIL

Translation and Contributions
DR. NASSER S. FARAG

Nordskog Publishing inc.

Ventura, California
2011

The Virgin Mary In the Light of The Word of God
by Dr. Labib Mikhail

First Edition, Arabic, 2006

Second Edition, Spanish, 2009

Third Edition, English, 2011
Translated and Contributions by Dr. Nasser S. Farag

Published by Nordskog Publishing Inc.

Copyright © 2011 by Labib Mikhail

International Standard Book Number: 978-0-9827074-9-4
Library of Congress Control Number: 2011923120

Manuscript and Theology Editor, Ronald W. Kirk
Proofreaders, Nola Grunden and Kimberley Woods

Design and Production by Desta Garrett, Managing Editor

Cover Painting, "Joy of the Harvest" by Simon Dewey
Courtesy Altus Fine Art, altusfineart.com

For information:

Nordskog Publishing, Inc.
2716 Sailor Avenue, Ventura, California 93001, USA
1-805-642-2070 • 1-805-276-5129 • www.NordskogPublishing.com

MEMBER

Christian Small Publishers Association

Dedication

There are two liberties in life.

One is from the slavery of sin.

> Jesus answered them, "Most assuredly, I say to
> you, whoever commits sin is a slave of sin....
> Therefore if the Son makes you free, you shall
> be free indeed." (John 8:34, 36)

The second freedom is that from human philosophies
and religions and, ultimately, from the civil state, as well
as from humanistic traditions within the Christian church.
Such external tyrannies impede the Gospel work and the
cause of Christ.

> Then Jesus said to those Jews who believed Him,
> "If you abide in My word, you are My disciples
> indeed. And you shall know the truth, and the
> truth shall make you free." (John 8:31–32)

To those who have received both stages of freedom, or
are longing to receive them...

I dedicate this book.

Rev. Dr. Labib Mikhail

A Word of Tribute from the Author

*S*alib *Farag* was a humble Christian layman whom the Lord put in my way when I was 16 years old attending a traditional church in my home country of Egypt. Having been brought up to believe and practice the devotion to and adoration of the blessed virgin Mary, I had accepted that without question.

In a process that is too lengthy to detail here, Brother Salib helped me start on a journey in which I came to know personally Jesus Christ as my only Savior and Mediator, and to spend my life studying and teaching the Word of God. This book is an outgrowth of my determined effort to know what the Scriptures reveal about *Jesus* and His blessed mother, the virgin *Mary*.

Brother Salib had also made a similar journey of faith. He was one of the first printers/publishers of Christian literature in the Arab world, printing, among other things, many of my early writings in the Arabic language.

After Brother Salib's departure to be with the Lord, I have come to consider his son, Nasser, as my adopted spiritual son in the Lord. Nasser, who has served as a missionary for forty-five years in Africa and Latin America and as a professor of missions in the U.S., contacted me after reading this book in Arabic. He shared that the book's message was urgently needed in Africa and Latin America where nominal Christianity is at times only a thin veneer over-lying deeply embedded native pagan beliefs and practices. He asked if he might translate it into English and Spanish and adapt it for use where needed throughout the world.

After prayer together, we completed the Spanish in 2009, and now the English edition as an additional witness to clarify the place of blessed Mary as taught in the Bible *for the Glory of GOD in CHRIST.*

Dr. Labib Mikhail
January, 2011

Contents

Foreword

AN URGENT CHALLENGE TO CHRISTIANITY

Father, Son, and Mother Mary—The Triune God!
What? Who believes this?
Why? Where? When?
How did it affect religious history?
Whom does it affect today?

*Y*ES, some Christian cults at the time in which the prophet of Islam lived—A.D. 570–625—had these unscriptural beliefs concerning the nature of Jesus, the Son of God, and the mother of Jesus, God in the flesh.

It is true that some so-called Christians who were not familiar with the Scriptures and were deceived by Satan went into a cultic belief that the Trinity consisted of Father God, Mother Mary, and their Son, Jesus. Islam rightly rejected this as their Quran states, "He is the Originator of the heavens and the earth. How can He have children when He has no wife?" (Surah 6:101, *The Quran Translation* by M.H. Shakir).

Their belief is that God dictated the Quran to their

prophet through the angel Gabriel, the *same* angel who spoke to the virgin Mary and told her of Jesus' miraculous birth. While the Quran supports the virgin birth of Jesus (whom they call the Prophet Isa), it also teaches that God (Allah) is a solitary person, who cannot be three persons in One.

Their logical conclusion, based on their belief that both Mary (whom they call Maryam) and Jesus (whom they call Isa) were 100 percent human, was that Christians were, therefore, insulting the One and Only True God by adding them alongside *Him*.

The traditional churches have always asserted that this is a distortion of their teachings. Nevertheless, their doctrine of elevating and praying to blessed Mary as the "Mother of God," and as an interceder and mediator, has caused confusion. It unintentionally feeds into a generalization that Christianity is an apostate religion believing in three gods. In the Quran we find this verse:

> And when Allah will say: O Isa son of Maryam! Did you say to men, Take me and my mother for two gods besides Allah, he will say: Glory be to Thee, it did not befit me that I should say what I had no right to [say]. (Surah 5:116, Shakir)

Muslims conclude and judge Christianity by the Quranic argument that *God is not born and does not give birth* (Surah 112:3, Shakir).

Because they also believe that children are automatic adherents to the religion of their father, they consider every so-called Christian or one who comes from a so-called Christian father to be a Christian. They do not *distinguish* between someone baptized as a child but who now rarely attends church and someone who has personally received and accepted the grace of Christ's salvation and has a living faith.

Many members of their religion notice multitudes of those whom they consider to be true Christians praying to blessed Mary or to God/Christ through Mary, and kneeling to her statue in adoration. It is easy to see how they justify their belief that Christianity is a pagan religion that worships two human beings (Mary/Maryam and her son, Jesus/Isa) in addition to God/Allah. They believe that they, not Christians, are following God's words when He commanded:

> You shall have no other gods before Me.... You shall not make for yourself a carved image—any likeness of anything...you shall not bow down to them nor serve them. For I...am a jealous God. (Exodus 20:3–5)

Islam teaches that Jesus was born by the Spirit of God, but is still merely a human prophet empowered by God's Spirit. To them He is not God in the flesh. This conclusion has helped convince and move some away from a belief in traditional Christianity to a belief in Islam. This has been evident over the past fourteen centuries, especially in Africa, Europe, and the Middle East.

Today, many from this religion (especially Arabs and Asians) are moving to Europe and the Americas (North and Latin), where they find good educational, business, and employment opportunities. They are increasing rapidly in these areas, not only through immigration but also through marriage to nominal Christians and through high birth rates. This becomes obvious in large cities like London, Paris, Berlin, Rome, Los Angeles, Sao Paulo, and Mexico City.

As we served in Latin America, we, along with everyone else including the followers of Islam, noticed the multitudes of so-called Christians who never attend church and whose lives do not portray a personal relationship with the Almighty God. Yet at the same time, they would spend tremendous time, energy, and money participating in specific feasts, festivals, and religious parades that clearly elevate Mary as an object of worship. Some would even crawl for hundreds of yards on their knees by the Basilica in Mexico City to reach and to show devotion to a special icon of blessed Mary.

In our ministry's evangelical center for missions on a Caribbean lagoon, we invited over 100 youth from a traditional church that we thought would be open to the

Gospel. We were happy to share the facility with them and to, hopefully, share Christ as well. To our disappointment, we and our team were not allowed to share the Gospel in the ministry's Casa para Cristo (House for Christ). On the contrary we were asked to join in what we assumed was the birthday party of one of their members. To our shock, we found written on the huge (3 ft. by 5 ft.) birthday cake, these words: "To Jesus through Mary" and "To Mary through Jesus." Thus, they were elevating blessed Mary as equal to or above Jesus.

In Africa, we noticed that some of the old ancestor-worship practices were still being included in the funerals and burial practices conducted by priests of traditional churches. It seems that these practices originally entered the church because the missionaries from an outside culture were unaware of their anti-Biblical meanings. Nevertheless, when their meanings become clear, there is no excuse for Christians to continue them.

Instead of labeling these people and churches as pagans and idol worshipers (as many evangelical ministers in Latin America do), we must do what Dr. Mikhail is doing, which is to teach the Word of God, which is the *Sword of the Spirit* (Ephesians 6:17). We need to reach out in love to our brothers and sisters from the traditional churches.

Our prayer is that all Christians will recognize the necessity of focusing on the Lordship of the unique and supreme Incarnate Son of God, our Savior Jesus Christ. Let us first proclaim Him in our own hearts, then to others, as the *only* Savior and Mediator between God and man (Acts 4:12; 1 Timothy 2:5). If we do this, not only does God save us unto eternal life, but He hampers Satan from using us as *obstacles*. We then help free non-believers to understand the essentials of the Christian faith. In fact, our stand of loyalty to the teachings of the Bible in contrast to loyalty to the teachings of men could be a stepping-stone toward leading many others, even from other belief systems, to live for Him.

I am deeply grateful to Dr. Labib Mikhail for allowing me to translate his Arabic book into English and Spanish, and for allowing me to make additions, deletions, and adaptations that address the situation of pertinent Catholic beliefs about blessed Mary as I experienced them in Latin America, the Caribbean, and Africa south of the Sahara. Thus this message virtually becomes relevant to Christians worldwide, including concerned evangelicals.

Dr. Nasser S. Farag
Translator and Contributor
English Edition

Introduction

*L*ET me first express that I believe that God blessed the
virgin Mary. As the angel Gabriel told her: "[B]lessed
are you among women!" (Luke 1:28). This was his greeting
when he came to announce that she would become pregnant
and give birth to a son, Jesus. It is also true that the virgin
Mary is a blessed woman for all peoples throughout time,
in the sense that all generations have called her "blessed."
This was her testimony:

> My soul magnifies the Lord, and my spirit has
> rejoiced in God my Savior. For He has regarded
> the lowly state of His maidservant; for behold,
> henceforth all generations will call me blessed.
> (Luke 1:46–48)

And the *reason* for her blessing was,

> For He who is mighty has done great things for
> me, and holy is His name. (Luke 1:49)

The Bible records this honor of being blessed, but does not give Mary the other titles that were later given her by the traditional churches. Therefore, my reason for writing this book is to give the reader who is searching for the truth the clear picture that the Holy Scriptures give about blessed Mary. I am urging the honest person to actively search for the truth by examining what the Bible says, regardless of what he has learned from other teachings and traditions. Follow the example of the Jews of Berea to whom Paul preached: "[T]hey received the word with all readiness, *and searched the Scriptures daily* to find out whether these things were so. Therefore many of them believed" (Acts 17:11–12, *emphasis added*).

This is my hope and prayer from my heart and soul—that this book will become a reason for blessing and guidance for every reader.

Rev. Dr. Labib Mikhail
January, 2011, U.S.A.

CHAPTER ONE

Blessed Are You Among Women

*H*UNDREDS of years before the time of Mary, the prophet Isaiah predicted that a virgin would give birth to a son. He said,

> Therefore the Lord Himself will give you a sign:
> Behold, the virgin shall conceive and bear a Son,
> and shall call His name Immanuel. (Isaiah 7:14)

Therefore, the Apostle Matthew declared that this prophecy was literally fulfilled when the Angel Gabriel hundreds of years later announced to the virgin Mary that she would become pregnant and give birth to a son who was to be named Jesus. He said:

> So all this was done that it might be fulfilled which was spoken by the Lord through the prophet, saying: "Behold, the virgin shall be

3

with child, and bear a Son, and they shall call His name Immanuel," which is translated, "God with us." (Matthew 1:22–23)

By the inspiration of the Holy Spirit, Matthew gave the interpretation to the name *Immanuel* as "God with us," and so he pronounced by this fact the virgin birth. When the New Testament explains an Old Testament prophecy, *it verifies the truth!*

Now let us read together what the evangelist Luke recorded after he carefully followed what had taken place with the virgin Mary at the time of her pregnancy with Jesus. God sent the angel Gabriel to the elderly priest Zacharias, pronouncing to him that his elderly barren wife Elizabeth would give birth to a son who was to be named John. This son would prepare the people to receive the Lord whom they were anticipating. John was the one in whom Isaiah's prophecy would be fulfilled.

> The voice of one crying in the wilderness: "Prepare the way of the LORD; make straight in the desert a highway for our God.... The glory of the LORD shall be revealed, and all flesh shall see it together; for the mouth of the LORD has spoken." (Isaiah 40:3,5)

> In those days John the Baptist came preaching in the wilderness of Judea, and saying, "Repent,

for the kingdom of heaven is at hand!" For this is He who was spoken of by the prophet Isaiah, saying: "The voice of one crying in the wilderness: 'Prepare the way of the LORD; Make His paths straight.'" (Matthew 3:1–3)

Now in the sixth month the angel Gabriel was sent by God to a city of Galilee named Nazareth, to a virgin betrothed to a man whose name was Joseph, of the house of David. The virgin's name was Mary. And having come in, the angel said to her, "Rejoice, highly favored one, the Lord is with you; blessed are you among women!"

But when she saw him, she was troubled at his saying, and considered what manner of greeting this was. Then the angel said to her, "Do not be afraid, Mary, for you have found favor with God. And behold, you will conceive in your womb and bring forth a Son, and shall call His name JESUS. He will be great, and will be called the Son of the Highest; and the Lord God will give Him the throne of His father David. And He will reign over the house of Jacob forever, and of His kingdom there will be no end."

Then Mary said to the angel, "How can this be, since I do not know a man?"

And the angel answered and said to her, "The

Holy Spirit will come upon you, and the power of the Highest will overshadow you; therefore, also, that Holy One who is to be born will be called the Son of God. Now indeed, Elizabeth your relative has also conceived a son in her old age; and this is now the sixth month for her who was called barren. For with God nothing will be impossible." (Luke 1:26–37)

In this sacred scene, Eternity met time and the Spiritual world met with man!

In the sixth month after Elizabeth conceived their son John, who became known as the Baptizer, the angel Gabriel came to the virgin Mary who was betrothed to a man from King David's lineage whose name was Joseph. He greeted her with the words:

"Rejoice, highly favored one, the Lord is with you; blessed are you among women!" (Luke 1:28)

Some people have objected to the phrase "blessed are you," and prefer the statement "full of blessing"; but in reality, there is no difference. After all, all blessings are from God. The angel Gabriel said to the virgin Mary, *you are blessed among women.*

Without any doubt, the virgin Mary was the most blessed woman whom God chose by His grace from all women in the world in which to conceive this Son who was to save the world. This is what the Apostle Paul said:

> But when the fullness of the time had come, God sent forth His Son, born of a woman, born under the law. (Galatians 4:4)

What a Godly blessing it was to be *that* woman!

Mary was troubled by Gabriel's words and wondered what did this mean. Without doubt, *this situation caused her fear and trembling.* The angel continued his words to remove her anxiety:

> Then the angel said to her, "Do not be afraid, Mary, for you have found favor with God. And behold, you will conceive in your womb and bring forth a Son, and shall call His name Jesus. He will be great, and will be called the Son of the Highest; and the Lord God will give Him the throne of His father David. And He will reign over the house of Jacob forever, and of His kingdom there will be no end." (Luke 1:30–33)

Gabriel's words pronounced the true nature of the child to whom the virgin Mary was to give birth. He is *The Son of the Highest*, and this king would rule forever with no one ever able to end his rule. What a fulfillment this would be of Daniel's prophecy in Daniel 7:13–14!

I was watching in the night visions, and behold, *One* like the Son of Man, coming with the clouds of heaven! He came to the Ancient of Days, and they brought Him near before Him. Then to Him was given dominion and glory and a kingdom, that all peoples, nations, and languages should serve Him. His dominion is an everlasting dominion, which shall not pass away, and His kingdom *the one* which shall not be destroyed.

At this point, it seems that Mary's mind was preparing a rational question. She was a virgin untouched by any man, so her question to the angel was, "How can this be, since I do not know a man?" (Luke 1:34). This question leaves no doubt that she had had no sexual contact with any man.

And the angel answered and said to her, "The Holy Spirit will come upon you, and the power of the Highest will overshadow you; therefore, also, that Holy One who is to be born will be called the Son of God." (Luke 1:35)

By these words, Gabriel pronounced to Mary that *the pregnancy would be by the Holy Spirit* and that God's power would protect her all through her pregnancy, and that the child to be born from her would be *His* Son, planned and arranged by God.

> Therefore, when He came into the world, He said:
> "Sacrifice and offering You did not desire, but a
> body You have prepared for Me." (Hebrews 10:5)

The angel informed Mary that her relative Elizabeth was also pregnant with a son in her old age because "with God nothing shall be impossible."

Mary, responding with such a powerful assurance of faith that it removed fear from her heart concerning what people would say when they would see her pregnant before marriage, said, "Behold the maidservant of the Lord! Let it be to me according to your word." (Luke 1:38)

Note that the word "handmaid" means *a servant* or *slave*. This was how the blessed virgin Mary accepted her role, in complete submission to God's will.

Mary quickly traveled to visit Elizabeth and as she entered the priest Zacharias' home the babe inside Elizabeth started moving (Luke 1:41–45). How could this happen? Does the fetus express feelings while still inside the womb? Remember that Gabriel had told Zacharias what the babe John would be:

> But the angel said to him, ... "For he will
> be great in the sight of the Lord, and shall
> drink neither wine nor strong drink. He will
> also be filled with the Holy Spirit, even from
> his mother's womb." (Luke 1:15)

9

Here is the first blessing received by the virgin Mary as expressed by Elizabeth in her greeting—through the Holy Spirit:

> Then she spoke with a loud voice saying, "Blessed are you among women, and blessed is the fruit of your womb! But why is this granted to me, that the mother of my Lord should come to me? For indeed, as soon as the voice of your greeting sounded in my ears, the babe leaped in my womb for joy. Blessed is she who believed, for there will be a fulfillment of those things which were told her from the Lord." (Luke 1:42–45)

All generations of true believers agree that Mary is blessed among women because she was the vessel that God the Father used to prepare the body of His Son, Jesus Christ, who would complete by His death on the cross God's plan for man's salvation. The virgin Mary is blessed among women because she believed in the possibility of this most unprecedented event in all human history...that a virgin girl can give birth without being touched by a man.

Now let us look at the specific words of Elizabeth that have caused a lot of controversy.... "But why is this granted to me, that the mother of my Lord should come to me?" (Luke 1:43). The traditional churches have built on these words of Elizabeth the teaching that Mary is the *Mother of*

God.[1] So what was the intention of the Holy Spirit when these words were recorded in Scripture?

It is logical that any mother precedes her son as far as time is concerned; but is that the case as far as the relation between Mary and Jesus? Did Mary precede Jesus as far as time? Certainly not! In fact, Christ was eternal with God the Father before creation.

> In the beginning was the Word, and the Word
> was with God, and the Word was God. (John 1:1)

Why then did the Holy Spirit record the words of Elizabeth? The reason is to confirm that the child who was to be born of Mary is God the Son incarnated. It is against all logic to try to make Mary, who was created in time the mother of the Eternal Son of God. Jesus is divine: Mary is human.

For nine months, Mary's body housed the child, Jesus, who in truth was the Lord of both Mary and Elizabeth. Humanly, Mary's womb nurtured the full humanity of her Lord, but she cannot be called the mother of His godly nature, which was eternally existent as the Second Person of the Triune God. In that respect, *He was her creator who*

---

1 Iris H. ElMasry, *Introduction to the Coptic Church* (Cairo, Egypt: Dar El Alam El Arabi, 1977), 49, and Most Rev. John Francis Noll, D.D., LL.D. and Rev. Lester J. Fallon, C.M., S.T.D., *Father Smith Instructs Jackson* (Huntington, Indiana: Our Sunday Visitor Press, 1960), 206.

See also: The Chalcedonian Creed AD 451, which orthodox Protestants accept; Mary as "the Mother of God" is sometimes translated as "the God-bearer."

preceded her before the world was made (Colossians 1:16). The divine baby Jesus, the Second Person in the Triune Godhead, is the Creator of His earthly mother, the virgin Mary, as John confirmed:

> *All* things were made through Him, and without Him nothing was made that was made. (John 1:3)

Christ was with the Father from the beginning and was sent by God in the fullness of time as Paul said:

> But when the fullness of the time had come, God sent forth His Son, born of a woman, born under the law, to redeem those who were under the law, that we might receive the adoption as sons. (Galatians 4:4–5)

The Apostle Paul in this verse mentions blessed Mary as "a woman," without any special prestigious label such as those given her by some traditional churches. According to this bright light of revelation, we again ask, "Why, then, did the Holy Spirit put these words on the lips of Elizabeth?" The answer is that the Holy Spirit intended that the words of Elizabeth clearly distinguish between the child in her own womb and the *One* who was in the womb of the virgin Mary, who was the Messiah.

> As it is written in the book of the words of Isaiah the prophet, saying: "The voice of one crying in

the wilderness: 'Prepare the way of the LORD; Make His paths straight. Every valley shall be filled and every mountain and hill brought low; the crooked places shall be made straight and the rough ways smooth; And all flesh shall see the salvation of God.'" (Luke 3:4–6)

John was a mere human being filled with the Holy Spirit. In contrast, Jesus is God in the flesh; He is God's salvation. Jesus is the one of whom David spoke in Psalm 27:1 and 35:3:

The LORD is my light and my salvation.
Say to my soul, "I am your salvation."

This unique agent of God's salvation was the Son of God and also the Son of Man incarnated in human flesh through the blessed virgin Mary.

CHAPTER TWO

The Agony of Doubt and the Comfort of Certainty

Our discussion turns here to Mary's fiancé, Joseph, as he moves from the agony of doubt to the comfort of certainty.

Mary stayed with her cousin Elizabeth about three months. When she returned home, Joseph must have noticed the change in her body due to the pregnancy, and it seems that Mary did not tell him of the angel's announcement. He must have begun doubting her purity and agonizing over his doubts. However, because he was a righteous man, he wanted to divorce her *secretly*.

Matthew recorded how the Lord removed the doubt from Joseph by sending His angel in a dream who revealed the truth about her pregnancy by the Holy Spirit. By this heavenly declaration, Joseph was set free from the agony of his suspicions about her innocence. This was exchanged by the certainty of her pure virginity. The cause of her pregnancy was nothing less than the Holy Spirit, Himself:

> Now the birth of Jesus Christ was as follows: After His mother Mary was betrothed to Joseph, before they came together, she was found with child of the Holy Spirit. Then Joseph her husband, being a just man, and not wanting to make her a public example, was minded to put her away secretly. But while he thought about these things, behold, an angel of the Lord appeared to him in a dream, saying, "Joseph, son of David, do not be afraid to take to you Mary your wife, for that which is conceived in her is of the Holy Spirit. And she will bring forth a Son, and you shall call His name JESUS, for He will save His people from their sins."
>
> So all this was done that it might be fulfilled which was spoken by the Lord through the prophet, saying: "Behold, the virgin shall be with child, and bear a Son, and they shall call His name Immanuel," which is translated, "God with us."
>
> Then Joseph, being aroused from sleep, did as the angel of the Lord commanded him and took to him his wife, and did not know her till she had brought forth her firstborn Son. And he called His name JESUS. (Matthew 1:18–25)

We can see clearly in these words that the Lord removed any doubt from Joseph concerning Mary's pregnancy. He removed all fear of marrying her as He told Joseph, "Do not be afraid to take Mary as your wife" (Matthew 1:20). Joseph did exactly what the angel said to him, and took Mary as his wife, but he did not *know her*—which means that he did not sleep with her, that he left her a virgin—until after she gave birth to Jesus, her firstborn son. The New American Standard Bible translates these verses as follows:

> And Joseph arose from his sleep, and did as the angel of the Lord commanded him, and took *her* as his wife, and *kept her a virgin* until she gave birth to a Son, and he called His name Jesus. (Matthew 1:24–25, NASB)

From these words, it is clear that Joseph did not touch Mary sexually *until* she gave birth to her first son. It was after the birth when they began sexual relations as an actual married couple. If that was not the case, why was the word "until" there..., saying that he did not sleep with her *until* she gave birth? The word *until* makes it clear that the period of no sexual relations was only until Jesus was born.

If Joseph did not "know" (have sexual relations with) Mary as a legitimate wife for him even *after* she gave birth to Jesus, that would have been recorded. The Scriptures are very clear about such important details as we can see

from what was written about King David and a virgin in
1 Kings 1:1–4:

> Now King David was old, advanced in years;
> and they put covers on him, but he could not
> get warm. Therefore his servants said to him,
> "Let a young woman, a virgin, be sought for our
> lord the king, and let her stand before the king,
> and let her care for him; and let her lie in your
> bosom, that our lord the king may be warm."
>
> So they sought for a lovely young woman
> throughout all the territory of Israel, and found
> Abishag the Shunammite, and brought her to
> the king. The young woman was very lovely; and
> she cared for the king, and served him; but the
> king did not know her.

In this situation, it is written that the king *did not know
her*, which means he *never* had sexual relations with her at
all. However, what is written about Joseph and Mary makes
it very clear that Joseph knew or slept with her *after* she gave
birth to Jesus. In the light of the Word of God's teaching
on marriage, there is nothing to imply that Mary's normal
marital relations with Joseph after she gave birth to Jesus
Christ would lower her reputation or eliminate her purity.
Marriage is God's plan for man. It is God's arrangement in
a holy and honorable manner as we read in Hebrews 13:4:

Marriage is honorable among all, and the bed undefiled.

If one of us considers marriage to be something that is unclean and that spoils one's spiritual purity, he is calling Almighty God the initiator of man's spiritual defilement because *He* is the one who planned marriage and who attended and blessed that of Adam and Eve. To consider normal marital relations a sin is a *double error*, for God cannot be tempted with evil and neither does He tempt any man (James 1:13).

As we consider Joseph's marriage to Mary, we have to answer a very important question: "Why did the Lord arrange for Joseph to marry the virgin Mary?" The answer is that the Lord protected Mary from punishment of death by stoning because of her giving birth to a child without a husband. Also, our Lord loved Mary and blessed her. Marriage, particularly for the Hebrews, was a blessing and remaining single a curse (Judges 11).

It was very important as far as the Law of Moses that the girl should be a virgin before marriage, and you can imagine what would have happened to Mary if she had given birth to Jesus without marriage. Who would have believed her if she would have said that she was made pregnant by the Holy Spirit? The Lord decided in His wisdom that Joseph, a righteous man, would betroth Mary and ultimately marry her. When Mary gave birth to Jesus, His birth certificate said "Jesus, the son of Joseph." The evangelist Luke (Luke 3:23) later wrote these words:

> Now Jesus Himself began His ministry at about thirty years of age, being (as was supposed) the son of Joseph.

Those who were living at the time of Jesus said, isn't this the son of the carpenter? Isn't his mother called Mary? (Mark 6:3).

Here we must stop and express our great appreciation for the faith of Mary and her humble obedience to the Lord's will in a complete surrender. Even though she knew from the words of the Law of Moses what could happen to her, Mary answered the angel Gabriel,

> "Behold the maidservant of the Lord! Let it be to me according to your word." And the angel departed from her. (Luke 1:38)

Blessed Mary believed completely in the wisdom of God, which is above all human wisdom and who always gives His wisdom in the proper place and time. With this trust, all fear was removed from her heart. The wisdom of God was displayed in His revelation to Joseph in a dream not to fear taking Mary as his wife because the one who was inside her was by the Holy Spirit. Therefore, the virgin Mary gave birth to her firstborn Son, Jesus, under the protection of this righteous man, Joseph, who did not consummate their marriage until after her first child was born.

CHAPTER THREE

Scenes Surrounding the Birth of Jesus

*M*ANY scenes surrounded the birth of Jesus Christ from the virgin Mary as Luke recorded in Luke 2:1–51. Now let us study what the Holy Spirit wanted to reveal through the record of so many incidents surrounding Jesus' birth.

FIRST of all, the heart of the king is in the hand of the Lord. This we read in the Scriptures:

> The king's heart is in the hand of the LORD,
> Like the rivers of water; He turns it wherever
> He wishes. (Proverbs 21:1)

In order that the prophecy from the prophet Micah be fulfilled, the Lord moved the heart of the Roman emperor Caesar Augustus to give an order to take a census (Micah 5:2):

> But you, Bethlehem Ephrathah, though you
> are little among the thousands of Judah, yet
> out of you shall come forth to Me the One to

be Ruler in Israel, whose goings forth are from
of old, from everlasting.

So Joseph went with *his wife*, Mary, to Bethlehem to
be registered and,

> While they were there, the days were completed
> for her to be delivered. And she brought forth her
> firstborn Son, and wrapped Him in swaddling
> cloths, and laid Him in a manger, because there
> was no room for them in the inn. (Luke 2:6–7)

And so it was that the Lord demonstrated His sovereignty
over the hearts of the kings and over the events in history.

SECOND: Mary gave birth to her *firstborn* Son, not to her
only child.

These words from that second chapter of Luke clearly
tell us that Jesus was the virgin Mary's *firstborn*, but it does
not say that He was her *only* child or the *only* Son. When
it says her firstborn, the Word of God declared that Mary
would give *birth to other children later*, and this same blessed
Word of God gave us the names of those others who were
her children. This we will discuss later in more detail.

THIRD: The heavens announced the birth of Jesus Christ,
the Lord.

In this chapter's magnificent, heavenly scene, the angels
of the Lord proclaim to the shepherds the time of the birth

of the Savior who is Christ the Lord (Luke 2:8–14).

After this exciting scene, the shepherds went to Bethlehem and found Mary and Joseph and the child lying in a manger and they reported the words that had been told them about the Babe (Luke 2:17).

FOURTH: Mary, after giving birth to Jesus, needed to be purified according to the Law (Luke 2:22–24).

According to the Law of Moses, because the Babe, Jesus, had opened her womb, Mary needed to be purified. Jesus was born under the law and in and through Him, all the commandments of the law were fulfilled. He was circumcised eight days after His birth (Luke 2:21) according to God's command (Genesis 17:9–13). His mother gave birth to Him naturally as any other woman, and when her days of purification were completed, went up to Jerusalem. According to Moses' law, she and Joseph presented to the Lord the Son who had opened her womb. They also presented a sin offering to cover her purification from the blood of childbirth (according to Moses' law in Leviticus 12:1–7).

FIFTH: Faithful Israelites saw in the Babe, Jesus, the salvation of God (Luke 2:25–32).

Luke also tells us of a man called Simeon, who was in Jerusalem and whom the Holy Spirit had assured that he would not die until he had seen the Christ of the Lord. When the Spirit led him into the temple Simeon saw in the child whom he held in his arms, the salvation of God, and he said,

My eyes have seen Your salvation. (Luke 2:30)

Another blessed scene occurred when the aged prophetess Anna was rewarded for her service day and night to the Lord in the temple by also being present to see the Christ child. She recognized Him as the one to bring salvation to the nations and shared the good news with all those living in Jerusalem who were expecting God's salvation (Luke 2:36–38).

It is easy to understand when years later Peter, after walking and talking with the *adult* Jesus Christ, declared that He is the only Savior for mankind.

Nor is there salvation in any other, for there is
no other name under heaven given among men
by which we must be saved. (Acts 4:12)

Nevertheless, these two aged, faithful Israelites, Simeon and Anna, recognized by the power of the Holy Spirit that this newborn child, Jesus, is the Savior whom the Lord had prepared for all the nations and that He is the light of salvation for the nations and a glory to the people of Israel (John 4:22).

SIXTH: Jesus pronounced to Joseph and Mary that His Father is the Heavenly Father.

In this sixth scene, and the last one in this second chapter of Luke's Gospel, we read about the family's journey to Jerusalem to celebrate the Passover according to the law. Jesus was twelve years old at the time which means that Mary and Joseph lived at least for twelve years (which is not a short time) together. After the feast, Mary and Joseph started home thinking that Jesus was among the other children in the group. Unknown to them, Jesus had remained in Jerusalem. Joseph and his wife Mary searched for Jesus among the other travelers, and when they did not find Him, they returned to Jerusalem.

> Now so it was that after three days they found Him in the temple, sitting in the midst of the teachers, both listening to them and asking them questions. And all who heard Him were astonished at His understanding and answers. So when they saw Him, they were amazed; and His mother said to Him, "Son, why have You done this to us? Look, Your father and I have sought You anxiously." (Luke 2:46–48)

At this time, Jesus pronounced to His mother Mary and His father Joseph that He is the Son of the Heavenly Father and that Joseph is not His true father.

> And He said to them, "Why did you seek Me? Did you not know that I must be about My Father's business?" (Luke 2:49)

Even though Mary should have known that Jesus was the son of the Heavenly Father because of what the angel Gabriel had told her—that He will be called the "Son of the Highest" (Luke 1:32), we see that Mary and Joseph did not understand Jesus' words:

> But they did not understand the statement which
> He spoke to them. (Luke 2:50)

In addition, Mary and Joseph did not know where Jesus was during those three days. If it had been within Mary's ability for her to know the unknown or unseen, she would not have been "amazed" and said to Jesus, "Son, why have You done this to us? Look, Your father and I have sought You anxiously" (Luke 2:48).

If blessed Mary had known where Jesus was, she would not have been searching and suffering because of His absence.

Luke paints for us these exciting scenes and then moves on to the even more exciting record of Jesus' life ministry of carrying out His Heavenly Father's business, and this business takes precedence over any earthly relationships, including that with His earthly mother.

CHAPTER FOUR

Look, Your Mother and Your Brothers

SOME people who follow certain traditions claim that Jesus' brothers, whose names are in the gospels of the New Testament, were not His brothers from blessed Mary but were His cousins instead. They have reached this state of denial because of the belief that the marital relationship is a relationship not fitting for Mary. They cite Song of Songs 4:12, Ezekiel 44:1–2, and other passages for support.[2] We showed in the previous chapter that this view is not Biblical.

We know from God's establishment and plan for marriage that Mary and Joseph's normal sexual marital relationship after she gave birth to Jesus was a clean and honorable marriage. We are assured by those who have carefully studied the Word of God that *Mary had a normal marriage with Joseph after she gave birth to Jesus*, and that she and Joseph

---

2 ElMasry, 48.

had several other children whose names we can read and can identify in the gospels.

THE NAMES OF JESUS' BROTHERS IN MATTHEW'S GOSPEL

When Jesus came back to His own area and began teaching in the synagogue, the people were surprised and said,

> Where did this Man get this wisdom and these
> mighty works? Is this not the carpenter's Son? Is
> not His mother called Mary? And His brothers
> James, Joses, Simon, and Judas? And His sisters,
> are they not all with us? Where then did this
> Man get all these things? (Matthew 13:54–56)

These words described the family according to the flesh from which Jesus came. He was known to be the son of Joseph the carpenter, and that His mother was Mary, and these brothers and sisters are through Mary and Joseph.

THE NAMES OF JESUS' BROTHERS IN THE GOSPEL OF MARK

Then He went out from there and came to His own country, and His disciples followed Him. And when the Sabbath had come, He began to teach in the synagogue. And many hearing Him were astonished, saying, "Where did this Man get these things? And what wisdom is this which is given

to Him, that such mighty works are performed
by His hands! Is this not the carpenter, the Son
of Mary, and brother of James, Joses, Judas, and
Simon? And are not His sisters here with us?"
So they were offended at Him. (Mark 6:1–3)

These words declare that Joseph was a carpenter and
that he had taught Jesus the profession of carpentry and
that is why Jesus was called "the carpenter." It is good to
notice that in both gospels, Mark and Matthew, the name
of His mother, Mary, and His brothers' names are linked
together. To be honest and forthright with the Word of
God, we should confess that the mentioning of Mary with
the names of the brothers means that His brothers are the
sons of Mary. Otherwise, why does the Holy Spirit connect
them with Him? Jesus was connected with His brothers
and tied to them by His mother in a very clear way that
no one can deny by saying they were His cousins unless
they want to change the Word of God.

Before we leave this discussion, we should remember that
the Apostle Paul mentioned in his epistle to the Galatians that
he had met in Jerusalem, James, one of the brothers of Jesus.

Then after three years I went up to Jerusalem to
see Peter, and remained with him fifteen days.
But I saw none of the other apostles except
James, the Lord's brother. (Galatians 1:18–19)

In Paul's words, James was the brother of the Lord, and this was the name of one of Mary's sons mentioned by both Matthew and Mark. Is it possible that the Apostle Paul would mention that James was the brother of the Lord when he was actually only the Lord's cousin? If Paul had made a mistake, would others who read Paul's writings and who knew the family not have corrected him?

ALSO, IN THE GOSPEL OF JOHN

We would note that during the time of the ministry of Jesus, His brothers did not believe in Him and challenged Him to show Himself.

> Now the Jews' Feast of Tabernacles was at hand. His brothers therefore said to Him, "Depart from here and go into Judea, that Your disciples also may see the works that You are doing. For no one does anything in secret while he himself seeks to be known openly. If You do these things, show Yourself to the world." For even His brothers did not believe in Him. (John 7:2–5)

This was the position of the brothers of Jesus who were actually from the same mother, Mary. They did not believe in Him; but after His resurrection, they knew the truth and James became a good, sound believer in His brother, Jesus. James, a son of Mary and the brother of Jesus, wrote

the epistle that bears his name—the Epistle of James.[3]
Another verse shows us Jesus' connection with His
brothers that the Apostle John mentioned.

> After this He went down to Capernaum, He,
> His mother, His brothers, and His disciples; and
> they did not stay there many days. (John 2:12)

The careful interpretation of the Word leads us to say,
that His brothers who went with Him and His mother
Mary to Capernaum were His brothers from Mary, *not*
His cousins. If not, why were they so many times with His
mother Mary? Why do we not see Jesus' aunt with them
since they evidently stayed there for some time?

Jesus was the firstborn to Mary, the oldest of her children, and the fact that He was going to Capernaum with
His mother and His brothers without Joseph means that
Joseph may have been dead by this time; and that Jesus
being the oldest was the one to take charge of the family
along with the mother.

I believe that Christians, faithful to the truth, would
after these Biblical examples, ask God to confirm to them
by the Holy Spirit if God's Word teaches that the "brothers"
of Jesus were His brothers from Mary and Joseph, even if
this disagrees with their church's traditions.

---

3 This conclusion is of a fair certainty. For documentation, see John Peter
Lange, *Commentary on the Holy Scriptures, Critical, Doctrinal, and Homiletical*
(Grand Rapids: Zondervan Publishing House, 1960), Volume 12, 9–12.

CHAPTER FIVE

My Brothers, My Sisters, And My Mother

*A*N old saying goes, "Try to convince a man against his will and he will stick to his position without retreat." This applies to the natural man, but the true Christian who has received God's salvation and the indwelling of the Holy Spirit accepts whatever God's Word says and refuses any traditions of men that contradict it. This is how the Apostle Paul expressed it:

> But the natural man does not receive the things of the Spirit of God, for they are foolishness to him; nor can he know them, because they are spiritually discerned. But he who is spiritual judges all things, yet he himself is rightly judged by no one. (1 Corinthians 2:14–15)

There is a very clear truth found in Jesus' words that the believers who do the Father's will are in the same position

33

and receive the same commendation as blessed Mary the mother of Jesus.

> While He was still talking to the multitudes, behold, His mother and brothers stood outside, seeking to speak with Him. Then one said to Him, "Look, Your mother and Your brothers are standing outside, seeking to speak with You."
>
> But He answered and said to the one who told Him, "Who is My mother and who are My brothers?" And He stretched out His hand toward His disciples and said, "Here are My mother and My brothers! For whoever does the will of My Father in heaven is My brother and sister and mother." (Matthew 12:46–50)

There are no clearer words than these that Jesus spoke to the masses while His mother and brothers were waiting outside wanting to talk to Him. The presence of His brothers with Mary shows that they were His true brothers. That Mary was waiting outside with her children perhaps meant that they were coming to tell Jesus about a family matter or seek His advice, since He, as the oldest son, was the head of the family. But when somebody came to tell Him of His family's presence outside, Jesus did not leave the masses and rush to meet His mother Mary. No! Look again at His response: "Who is My mother? and who are

My brethren?" (Matthew 12: 48, KJV, *caps added*).

He was again reinforcing the priority of His relationship to His Father in heaven rather than to a human family. Jesus answered His own question by stretching out His arm to include in His family *all* those who do God's will,

> and said, *"Here* are…My brother and sister and mother." (Matthew 12:49–50, *emphasis added*.)

Let us examine another situation found in Luke.

> And it happened, as He spoke these things, that a certain woman from the crowd raised her voice and said to Him, "Blessed is the womb that bore You, and the breasts which nursed You!"
> But He said, "More than that, blessed are those who hear the word of God and keep it!" (11:27–28)

The woman by her own words had already blessed Mary, the mother of Jesus. Yet Jesus answered that those are blessed who truly listen to the Word of God, believe and follow it. Jesus put those *who believe and follow the Word of God and act on it* in a position higher than the womb that carried Him and the breasts that fed Him.

Jesus said "more than that," which means "more properly" or "more correctly speaking," those who believe and keep the Word of God are the ones who are blessed. Christ had the ability to always focus on His mission in bringing people to belief in and obedience to God rather than to be sidetracked by less important issues, even if that included praise for His mother.

CHAPTER SIX

Woman, What Have I To Do with You?

W E cannot find in the four gospels one verse that shows Jesus addressing Mary as "Mother" or saying "My mother," but always He addresses her as "woman." This does not mean that He dishonored her, but it has great importance. We see in the Gospel of John the occasion of the first time where this is recorded:

> On the third day there was a wedding in Cana of Galilee, and the mother of Jesus was there. Now both Jesus and His disciples were invited to the wedding. And when they ran out of wine, the mother of Jesus said to Him, "They have no wine."
>
> Jesus said to her, "Woman, what does your concern have to do with Me? My hour has not yet come."
>
> His mother said to the servants, "Whatever He says to you, do it." (2:1-5)

Mary was at a wedding in which Jesus and His disciples were also invited. We know that the Jews used to serve wine on these occasions and the wine had been consumed. It seems that Mary did not understand clearly the reality of Jesus being God in the flesh. If she had known that, she would have known also that He already was aware that the wine was finished and the wedding family was in need of someone to save them from that embarrassing situation. She informed Him of the problem as if He did not know. Jesus answered her in a way so that she would understand that He was no longer under her and Joseph's direction (if he was still living) as He had been in early life as a child:

> Then He went down with them and came to Nazareth, and was subject to them. (Luke 2:51)

Those taught from non-Biblical sources to put Mary as a queen on the right hand of God in heaven ought to stop and reconsider when they hear Jesus' words: "Woman, what does your concern have to do with Me?" We see that Jesus' answer clearly did not give His mother any title like those with which these traditions have given her.

Certainly, the use of the word "woman" was not an insult to Mary, but it was a necessary correction in her understanding of Him and of His true relationship to her. He is her Son according to the flesh, but according to the Spirit, He was the Son of God from the beginning...before creation. She did not exist before Him; He is the pre-existent One, and she is just a part of time and history. We can see all of this in His question, "Woman, what does your concern have to do with Me?"

It is also obvious from Mary's words to the servants that she understood from Jesus' question that His position of deity, knowledge, and authority was completely different and higher than her earthly nature and position: "Whatever He says to you, do it" (John 2:5).

Something else very important in Jesus' answer to Mary were His words, "My hour has not yet come," which shows us that Jesus' actions were all done with complete and precise control...they were not a matter of haphazard accidents. We can also see this in John:

> Now before the Feast of the Passover, when Jesus knew that His hour had come that He should depart from this world to the Father, having loved His own who were in the world, He loved them to the end. (13:1)

And also in John:

> Jesus spoke these words, lifted up His eyes to heaven, and said: "Father, the hour has come. Glorify Your Son, that Your Son also may glorify You." (17:1)

After Jesus' words with His mother in Cana, the time came for Him to show His glory and, therefore, He did the miracle of changing the water into wine.

> This beginning of signs Jesus did in Cana of Galilee, and manifested His glory; and His disciples believed in Him. (John 2:11)

We need to understand that Jesus was the miracle-maker, and that Mary throughout her entire life never made any miracle. Whoever tries to attach to her miracle-making power after her death is making a serious blunder and creating confusion. The Scriptures never give one instance in which a dead saint made a miracle, even if that saint, such as Moses and Elijah, had performed miracles during his lifetime.

Another time we see Jesus calling His mother "Woman" was while He was on the cross and Mary was standing there with the disciple John.

> Now there stood by the cross of Jesus His mother, and His mother's sister, Mary the wife of Clopas, and Mary Magdalene. When Jesus therefore saw His mother, and the disciple whom He loved standing by, He said to His mother, "Woman, behold your son!" Then He said to the disciple, "Behold your mother!" And from that hour that disciple took her to his own home. (John 19:25–27)

The cross was the instrument by which the sword passed into Mary's soul, the sword of seeing her son hanging on the cross suffering from tremendous pain and agony. On the cross, Jesus gave His disciple John to Mary, because even up to the time of the crucifixion His brothers did not believe in Him, and that is why He said from the cross, "Woman, behold your son!" (John 19:26).

Let us think deeply what these words mean when Jesus called His mother "Woman." It is actually a fulfillment of the promise God gave to all mankind in the Garden of Eden when He cursed the serpent (Satan) and told him that even though he would war against the woman's seed (Jesus Christ), his (Satan's) head would be bruised (Satan would be defeated) by the seed of the woman (Jesus Christ).

> God said to the serpent, "...And I will put enmity between you and the woman, and between your seed and her Seed; He shall bruise your head, and you shall bruise His heel." (Genesis 3:15)

Jesus Christ was the only one who can be called "the Seed" or "descendent of a woman" because He was born from the virgin Mary without any seed from a man being involved in His conception. Mary is the woman whom God chose from all the women of the world, and He has blessed her through the One He sent to bless the world. Praise the Lord for His wisdom and grace!

41

CHAPTER SEVEN

Can Blessed Mary Be Another Mediator?

$\int$ OME traditional churches believe that Mary can mediate and intercede on our behalf to God.[4] Let us examine this teaching in light of the definition of a mediator. *Webster's New Collegiate Dictionary* says a mediator interposes between parties at variance to reconcile them. The word refers to someone who helps on behalf of another. Mediation means to appeal for help and forgiveness for those who are in need.

When two human beings are in need of mediation, another person might very well have the necessary qualifications to be their mediator. However, when one speaks about a mediator between Almighty God and man, the Bible states that there is only one mediator, Christ Jesus, who gave Himself a ransom for all (1 Timothy 2:5–6). Vine's says:

The salvation of men necessitated that the Mediator

---

4 ElMasry, 49, and Noll and Fallon, 206.

should Himself possess the nature and attributes of Him toward whom He acts, and should likewise participate with the nature of those for whom He acts (sin apart); only by being possessed both of deity and humanity could He comprehend the claims of the one and the needs of the other; further, the claims and the needs could be met only by One who, Himself being proved sinless, would offer Himself an expiatory sacrifice on behalf of men.[5]

The Book of Hebrews describes Christ as the only One who meets these conditions:

• He (he/she) should be righteous from his/her original nature. He should have been born righteous; he did not receive the original sin that all human beings have inherited from Adam (Hebrews 9:14; 7:26).

• He should be able to cover all sins by his own redemptive act or sacrifice (Hebrews 9:14–15).

• He should always be alive and present everywhere in order to be available to all men in all of history (Hebrews 7:25).

---

5 W. E. Vine, Merrill F. Unger, William White, Jr., *Vine's Complete Expository Dictionary of Old and New Testament Words* (Nashville: Thomas Nelson Publisher, 1996), 400.

ARE THESE CONDITIONS FOR A MEDIATOR FOUND IN BLESSED MARY?

• Was Mary born without sin; was she naturally righteous from her birth? If so, she would not be in need of a Savior. No, the Scriptures teach that *all* human beings have sinned:

> The LORD looks down from heaven upon the children of men, to see if there are any who understand, who seek God. They have all turned aside, they have together become corrupt; there is *none who does good, no, not one.* (Psalm 14:2–3)

And:

> For *all have sinned* and fall short of the glory of God. (Romans 3:23) (*Emphasis added.*)

Some churches believe the unbiblical teaching that Mary was born without sin, yet Mary never claimed to be without sin and she gave testimony that God was her Savior:

> And Mary said, "My soul magnifies the Lord, and my spirit has rejoiced in God my Savior." (Luke 1:46–47)

We know from God's Word that Jesus Christ was the only person who was born without sin in His own nature, and the only one who claimed that He was sinless:

> Jesus said to them, "...Can any of you prove Me guilty of sin?" (John 8:46, NIV)

For He made Him who knew no sin to be sin
for us, that we might become the righteousness
of God in Him. (2 Corinthians 5:21)

If anyone sins, we have an Advocate with the
Father, Jesus Christ the righteous. (1 John 2:1)

We have a great High Priest... Jesus the Son of
God... [who] was in all points tempted as we
are, yet without sin. (Hebrews 4:14–15)

Jesus was the only person who was able to pay the
penalty for our sins by giving His life on the cross as the
perfect sinless ransom:

He Himself is the propitiation for our sins, and
not for ours only but also for the whole world.
(1 John 2:2)

• Did Mary give herself as a sacrifice or as a ransom for
sin; did she shed her blood to cover our sins? No, Mary did
not die for our sins; she cannot ask the Father to forgive
us, because,

It is the blood that makes atonement for the
soul. (Leviticus 17:11)

Without shedding of blood there is no remis-
sion. (Hebrews 9:22)

• Can Mary be found all over the world? Can she hear

and answer the prayers of all people? No, it is only God who is omnipresent and has absolute power and knowledge. If Mary could hear the prayers of those who ask her to mediate for them, it would make her on the same level as God who is the only Absolute One.

Can you imagine that one person is praying in Australia, one in Athens, one in London, one in Mexico City, another in southern Argentina, and all of them are praying to Mary and asking her to mediate on their behalf? Is Mary present everywhere and does she hear all these prayers and requests? If we believe this, we are giving to Mary the attributes that belong *only* to God; and this is a blasphemy against *Him*. The Prophet Isaiah warns against believing such things:

> And when they say to you, "Seek those who are mediums and wizards, who whisper and mutter," should not a people seek their God? Should they seek the dead on behalf of the living? To the law and to the testimony! If they do not speak according to this word, it is because there is no light in them. (8:19–20)

The only mediator anywhere, everywhere, and at any and all times is the Resurrected, Eternally Present Christ.

> Therefore He [Christ] is also able to save to the uttermost those who come to God through Him,

since He always lives to make intercession for them. (Hebrews 7:25)

Jesus' own words were, "For where two or three are gathered together in My name, I am there in the midst of them" (Matthew 18:20), and "I am with you always, even to the end of the age" (Matthew 28:20).

However, Mary has completed the mission God had for her on earth and she is now at rest. She cannot help anyone here on earth except by her beautiful example for us to follow of faithful obedience and surrender to God's plan and will.

Let us look at a Biblical explanation about the contrast between a believer's condition while alive and then, after death. As Paul was facing death, he spoke to the issue of whether a dead person (even a saint) could continue to serve/labor for other believers (i.e. through intercessory prayer, encouragement, making miracles).

> For to me, to live is Christ, and to die is gain. But if I live on in the flesh, this will mean fruit from my labor; yet what I shall choose I cannot tell. For I am hard-pressed between the two, having a desire to depart and be with Christ, which is far better. Nevertheless to remain in the flesh is more needful for you. (Philippians 1:21–24)

Before going to heaven, Paul was ending his service on behalf of the saints who were living on earth. He realized that to stay alive in the body was better (would bring more advantages) for them than his presence in heaven. The reason is that once the saints have departed this earth to be with the Lord, their earthly mission has ended.

No one in heaven can help the living saints here on earth or can make miracles for them except our great High Priest Jesus Christ. This is the same case with all those, including Mary, who die in the Lord. This we see clearly in the case of Daniel, who, after the Lord had used him as a faithful witness and the spokesperson for relaying so many prophecies, was told,

> But you, go your way till the end; for you shall rest, and will arise to your inheritance at the end of the days. (Daniel 12:13)

No saint in heaven will have any relation with people of earth until the Second coming of Christ. Look at what Paul wrote to the saints in Thessalonica.

> But I do not want you to be ignorant, brethren, concerning those who have fallen asleep, lest you sorrow as others who have no hope. For if we believe that Jesus died and rose again, even so God will bring with Him those who sleep in Jesus.

For this we say to you by the word of the Lord, that we who are alive and remain until the coming of the Lord will by no means precede those who are asleep. For the Lord Himself will descend from heaven with a shout, with the voice of an archangel, and with the trumpet of God. And the dead in Christ will rise first. Then we who are alive and remain shall be caught up together with them in the clouds to meet the Lord in the air. And thus we shall always be with the Lord. Therefore comfort one another with these words. (1 Thessalonians 4:13–18)

Those who are laid to rest in Jesus, including Mary, the mother of Jesus, God will bring back with Him. It is only then that the faithful dead will have contact with the faithful living. But before that time, to talk about their appearing in this or that place, and they make this or that miracle, or they help those in need of assistance is completely contradictory to what is written in the Word of God.[6]

Related to this subject, we must answer an extremely important question: How did this doctrine of Mary's mediation enter the Christian church? From historical records, we understand that many persons having false teachings had entered the church even from the time of the apostles.

---

6 This is discussed more fully in Chapter Eleven.

Paul offered warnings about them in several places including Galatians.

> I marvel that you are turning away so soon from Him who called you in the grace of Christ, to a different gospel, which is not another; but there are some who trouble you and want to pervert the gospel of Christ. But even if we, or an angel from heaven, preach any other gospel to you than what we have preached to you, let him be accursed. (1:6–8)

In addition, Peter wrote,

> But there were also false prophets among the people, even as there will be false teachers among you, who will secretly bring in destructive heresies, even denying the Lord who bought them, and bring on themselves swift destruction. (2 Peter 2:1)

This is what John wrote:

> Little children, it is the last hour; and as you have heard that the Antichrist is coming, even now many antichrists have come, by which we know that it is the last hour. (1 John 2:18)

No doubt, there were many factions among the Christians

at the time of the apostles.[7] Paul and John mentioned these factions in their letters (e.g., 1 Corinthians 1:10–11; Titus 1:10–11). True Christians were persecuted repeatedly in several places in the Roman Empire. Even the church in Rome had to live underground in the catacombs for many years because persecution and death pursued them. The greater the persecution, the greater their faith grew until the year 315 when the Roman Emperor Constantine took power.

History tells us that during this time, Constantine was in a big struggle with another political opponent and during that war, he had a very strange vision. He saw a large fiery cross in the sky, on which was written in fiery letters the words: "With this, you will be victorious."[8] He believed in that vision and, therefore, accepted Christianity.

When Constantine overcame his enemy and became the Emperor of Rome, he ordered the cessation of the persecution of the church. In order to unite his empire politically and religiously, he made Christianity the state religion for the Empire. This error is typical of the kinds sinful men make in history. Instead of depending on the protection of the Lord, many Christians started depending

---

7 Augustus Neander, *General History of the Christian Religion and Church*, (London: Henry G. Bohn, 1851). Volume I possesses an excellent treatment of the factions, persecutions, and character of the church in the early era of the church, in "Section First, Relation of the Christian Church to the unchristian World," 95-247. Also, Williston Walker, *A History of the Christian Church*, 3rd Ed. (New York: Charles Scribner's Sons, 1970), 125.

8 Augustus Neander, *General History of the Christian Religion and Church*, Volume III. (London: Henry G. Bohn, 1851), 10.

on the power of the state. In addition, at this same time, the power and authority of the priesthood arose and, over time, this religious authority and power became centered in one or a few church leaders.

People from every direction came into the church, coming with pagan backgrounds and ungodly cultural practices. Even where they entered the church with true conversion, as with all of us, sanctifying change takes time. They brought error with them from their humanistic cultures. Many no doubt entered the church without having a personal relationship with Christ that would cause them to desire to draw close to God. They had no (or few) Scriptures in their languages and received little teaching from church leaders. Often, the church's leaders were in the process of defining their doctrines as well as competing among themselves for ecclesiastical authority, which left inadequate emphasis on the evangelism and discipleship of their members. Christian growth requires faith and seeking understanding from the Word, application and evaluation of the fruit. We make mistakes; this is normal. But such searching means sometimes introducing error. Moreover, some, as John cites above, are merely evil wolves seeking to mislead the sheep of Christ.[9]

For whatever reason, some of the pagan beliefs that the new peoples brought into the church included the practice

---

9 Neander. Volume I, 125.

of glorifying a human male or female deity, similar to stories they heard about blessed Mary. The ungrounded church accepted the large numbers who entered along with their backgrounds of unscriptural teachings. The church leaders, priests, and missionaries covered over many of these indigenous false teachings with misinterpretations of verses from the Bible in order to establish their authority over these new geographical regions and to increase the number of followers.

When a false teaching arises from the outside and is unveiled and studied, the careful Christian can easily expose it as an unscriptural error. However, if the false teaching is ignored, covered, or dressed up with half or partial truths to become a part of a religious system, it becomes a *holy heresy*. This is usually very difficult to confront, exposing to grave danger the person who tries to correct such systems. Such is the history of the Reformation, for example. History has shown that once a church allows false teaching to enter its system of beliefs, that church will often defend that false teaching to the death.

The teachings glorifying blessed Mary that entered the traditional churches spread throughout the world, causing many Christians to deviate from the Biblical truth. This has caused serious consequences both inside and outside the church.

You can understand the over-reaction from Mohammed and Islam (in the sixth and seventh centuries A.D.) which we read in the Quran, chapter 5:116, that Allah was unhappy that they (Christians) took Isa (Jesus) and his mother as two gods. Therefore, the popularity and spread of Islam had to do, among other things, with a reaction to the church's unbiblical teaching that put Mary almost on the same level with God. The false teachings glorifying blessed Mary have had a long-term effect on 1.5 billion Muslims alive today, as well as those who lived in the past.

While some unbiblical teachings may have originated from good motives, over time they become strongholds that bind the minds of their followers with dark chains preventing the eyes from seeing the true light. Take for example the story of the brass serpent that Moses made in the wilderness.

> Then they journeyed from Mount Hor by the way of the Red Sea, to go around the land of Edom; and the soul of the people became very discouraged on the way.
>
> And the people spoke against God and against Moses: "Why have you brought us up out of Egypt to die in the wilderness? For there is no food and no water, and our soul loathes this worthless bread."
>
> So the LORD sent fiery serpents among the people, and they bit the people; and many of the people of Israel died.

Therefore the people came to Moses, and said, "We have sinned, for we have spoken against the LORD and against you; pray to the LORD that He take away the serpents from us." So Moses prayed for the people.

Then the LORD said to Moses, "Make a fiery serpent, and set it on a pole; and it shall be that everyone who is bitten, when he looks at it, shall live."

So Moses made a bronze serpent, and put it on a pole; and so it was, if a serpent had bitten anyone, when he looked at the bronze serpent, he lived. (Numbers 21:4–9)

We can see that God intended the bronze serpent to teach salvation comes through simple, obedient faith. It was clear that the serpent itself had no ability, it was just a piece of brass shaped into the form of a serpent; but God asked Moses to raise it up in order to test the faith of his people. The Lord Jesus explained this in his talk with Nicodemus:

And as Moses lifted up the serpent in the wilderness, even so must the Son of man be lifted up: That whosoever believeth in Him should not perish, but have eternal life. (John 3:14–15)

Therefore, the purpose for making this serpent was to demonstrate that obedient faith gives life; but as the days passed, the people forgot the original purpose even though it is recorded in the inspired Word of God (Numbers 21:9). People started to honor this brass serpent and even make offerings and burn fires to it (2 Kings 18:4); and thus the brass serpent itself became a *holy heresy*. It was not that easy for the Israelites to fight this because it was not just a false teaching coming from the outside; it came from within the religious system and was a part of their history and teachings.

The people needed a reformer to uncover the truth behind these *holy heresies* to point out their falseness, and to destroy them in front of the people's eyes, just as Hezekiah the great reformer King did.

> He removed the high places and broke the sacred pillars, cut down the wooden image and broke in pieces the bronze serpent that Moses had made; for until those days the children of Israel burned incense to it, and called it Nehushtan.
> (2 Kings 18:4)

This is a clear example of how the serpent which originally was a symbol declaring the power of obedient faith, through time became a *holy heresy—a stumbling block to the faith.*

Throughout Christian history, there have been errors, both theological and cultural, and deviations from the

Scriptures in every church, including those bearing the name of Protestant, Evangelical, and Charismatic. May we undertake self-examination, be confessional, and be ready to change unbiblical beliefs when we fall short.

In the beginning, some of the teachings were only meaningful for some persons from certain cultural backgrounds. However, through time, they were accepted without question by the majority of those growing up in these churches, and are even defended to the death—spiritually or physically.

God blessed Mary among women and all the generations bless her accordingly. She is an excellent example for every man and woman to follow in her complete surrender to God's will that she would become the honored and pure vessel that would carry the Lord Jesus, regardless of what difficulties she would be exposed to. This is her status and stature in the declarations of the New Testament. We cannot go further and attribute more, lest we impose on this blessed woman of humility something that Mary herself would have refused had she, when she was here on earth, known what was to happen in the future.

CHAPTER EIGHT

Was Blessed Mary Assumed[10] Bodily Into Heaven?

NOTHING can be found in the Bible that would support a traditional church's teaching that the body of blessed Mary was assumed up into heaven.[11] It is very strange that some believe that to be true. If it were true, why does the Bible not mention anything about such an event?

In fact, many teachings we hear concerning Mary cannot be found in the Bible and are not consistent with the teachings of the apostles and original followers of Christ. We can turn especially to the Apostle John to learn about Mary, he whom Jesus loved and to whom Jesus had said from the cross, "Behold your mother."

John was the one disciple that surely must have known blessed Mary better than any other New Testament writer except James, Jesus' brother. What catches our attention is

---

10 See "Bodily Assumption," Lexicon, p. 129.
11 ElMasry, 49, and Noll and Fallon, 210.

that although he must have lived much longer than Mary did and would have known all the details of her death since she was dwelling in his home, yet, John does not give any support for these extra-Biblical elevations of Mary. In his epistles, John did not write one word whatsoever about Mary in contrast to other women in the church whom he mentioned (2 John 1).

We would ask why the Bible would mention the Prophet Elijah's assumption (2 Kings 2:1-15), but never say anything about the body of blessed Mary. If the Lord wanted Mary's body to be assumed up after death, why did He not just translate her to heaven without her seeing death[12] as He did with Enoch (Genesis 5:24) and the prophet Elijah?

We would also ask with what kind of body was Mary assumed. Was it the physical body with which she was born? The Scriptures teach us that this is impossible:

> Now this I say, brethren, that flesh and blood cannot inherit the kingdom of God; nor does corruption inherit incorruption.
>
> (1 Corinthians 15:50)

The Word of God tells us that when Moses asked to see His face, the Lord said, "For no man shall see Me, and live" (Exodus 33:20).

---

12 While most believe that Mary did die, there are a few who think she was assumed bodily into heaven before death.

If one says that Mary was assumed up with a glorified body, this is contrary to the New Testament's revelation that we will not receive a glorified body until the second coming of Christ. The Bible mentions only one person—Jesus—rising to heaven with a glorified body, and He, as God in the flesh, ascended by His own power.

> For our citizenship is in heaven, from which we also eagerly wait for the Savior, the Lord Jesus Christ, who will transform our lowly body that it may be conformed to His glorious body, according to the working by which He is able even to subdue all things to Himself.
>
> (Philippians 3:20–21)

Therefore, this doctrine of Mary's assumption to heaven has no support in the Word of God, and intends to give blessed Mary a position that the Lord did not give her in His Word. The Lord in His wisdom intended not to mention in the New Testament when Mary died or where she was buried so that people would not go there to make it a shrine, turning their eyes from the Lord to one of His creatures.

In the Old Testament, the Lord in His wisdom intended the same thing regarding Moses' burial site. There was no doubt that the prophet Moses was a unique and most blessed prophet.

But since then there has not arisen in Israel a prophet like Moses, whom the LORD knew face to face. (Deuteronomy 34:10)

No one can ignore Moses' position with God and the people. After Aaron and Miriam spoke against Moses, the Lord said,

Hear now My words: "If there is a prophet among you, I, the LORD, make Myself known to him in a vision; and I speak to him in a dream. Not so with My servant Moses; he is faithful in all My house. I speak with him face to face, even plainly, and not in dark sayings; and he sees the form of the LORD. Why then were you not afraid to speak against My servant Moses?" (Numbers 12:6–8)

Through Moses, the Lord made many miracles and wonderful signs.

But since then there has not arisen in Israel a prophet like Moses, whom the LORD knew face to face, in all the signs and wonders which the LORD sent him to do in the land of Egypt, before Pharaoh, before all his servants, and in all his land, and by all that mighty power and all the great terror which Moses performed in the sight of all Israel. (Deuteronomy 34:10–12)

However, when it was time for Moses to die, his funeral was unique:

> Then Moses went up from the plains of Moab to Mount Nebo.... And the LORD showed him all the land of Gilead as far as Dan.... Then the LORD said to him, "This is the land of which I swore to give Abraham, Isaac, and Jacob, saying, 'I will give it to your descendants.' I have caused you to see it with your eyes, but you shall not cross over there."
>
> So Moses the servant of the LORD died there in the land of Moab, according to the word of the LORD. And He buried him in a valley in the land of Moab, opposite Beth Peor; but no one knows his grave to this day. (Deuteronomy 34:1, 4–6)

So why did the Lord hide Moses' place of burial? Why did not the Lord allow him to die among his people so they could bury him in a place they could know and return there to make a pilgrimage? The Lord did not want them to continue looking to Moses after he died, taking him as a mediator, presenting him gifts and offerings, and coming to him with their needs and troubles instead of to God. God did the same thing with the blessed Mary.

The Lord knows men's hearts, that they are deceitful and also are easily deceived and deviated from the truth:

> The heart is deceitful above all things, and desperately wicked; who can know it? I, the LORD, search the heart, I test the mind, even to give every man according to his ways, according to the fruit of his doings. (Jeremiah 17:9–10)

Not the prophet Moses nor the blessed Mary—the Lord wants to be the *only* One to whom people come as their refuge and with their songs of praise:

> God is our refuge and strength, a very present help in trouble. (Psalm 46:1)

> Look to Me, and be saved, all you ends of the earth! For I am God, and there is no other. (Isaiah 45:22)

After hundreds of years, Moses came to the Mount of Transfiguration with Elijah and Jesus (Matthew 17:1-8). The disciples witnessed this reappearance of Moses and Elijah from heaven to fellowship with Jesus only one time and then only to bring glory to Christ. They appeared only in the presence of Christ when God's voice testified to the Son that He alone deserved honor. These facts are quite different from what happens when people say that the blessed Mary has reappeared.

Peter's response to the Transfiguration was that he wanted to make three tabernacles for them, but the Heavenly Father refused to share the glory of the Beloved Son with any other person, even with these wonderful prophets. Peter must have thought that Jesus needed the assistance of these wonderful saints, just as people today want the departed saints to share a portion of the Lord Jesus' ministry of salvation, intercession, and sanctification. However, God's response today is the same as his response to Peter:

> [S]uddenly a voice came out of the cloud, saying, "This is My beloved Son, in whom I am well pleased. Hear Him!" (Matthew 17:5)

The Lord removed Elijah and Moses so that when the disciples raised their eyes they could see no one except Jesus. They did listen to Jesus, and His words repeated this same message:

> Jesus said unto them again, "...I am the door. If anyone enters by Me, he will be saved, and will go in and out and find pasture." (John 10:9)

> Jesus said to him, "I am the way, the truth, and the life. No one comes to the Father except through Me....
>
> "And whatever you ask in My name, that I will do, that the Father may be glorified in the Son. If you ask anything in My name, I will do it." (John 14:6, 13–14)

So it is only the Lord Jesus Christ who is the door for salvation, He is the only way to the Father, His name is the only name in which we pray, and He is the one who strengthens us and answers prayer.

Let us look at the teachings of the first Apostles, who taught by the Holy Spirit, concerning our Mediator. Listen to what Paul says:

> For there is one God and one Mediator between
> God and men, the Man Christ Jesus, who gave
> Himself a ransom for all. (1 Timothy 2:5–6)

The Apostle Paul said very clearly in these two verses that there is One Mediator, the man Jesus Christ. He calls Him "the man" so any man would not feel weak or afraid in coming to Him. He negates or denies the presence of any other mediators because Christ is the only one who gave His life as a ransom for all. No saint in the New Testament or in history has given his life as a ransom for all.

Here is what the Apostle John says on the subject:

> My little children, these things I write to you,
> so that you may not sin. And if anyone sins, we
> have an Advocate with the Father, Jesus Christ
> the righteous. And He Himself is the propitia-
> tion for our sins, and not for ours only but also
> for the whole world. (1 John 2:1–2)

John assures us that our mediator with the Father is Jesus Christ the righteous. As we have said before, no one can stand before a holy God as a mediator unless his original nature is righteous. Yet we know that all humans are unrighteous:

> There is none righteous, no not one.
> (Romans 3:10)

> For all have sinned and fall short of the glory
> of God. (Romans 3:23)

Regardless of how holy a person is, whatever the person did for Jesus, or whatever pain he suffered for the sake of Jesus, his original nature is still not righteous and he cannot mediate between God and man. For that reason, there is no other way to go to God except through the only mediator, the righteous Jesus Christ.

The Apostle Peter, the one who learned the eternal lesson on the Mount of Transfiguration, preached the good news that:

> Nor is there salvation in any other, for there is
> no other name under heaven given among men
> by which we must be saved. (Acts 4:12)

Why is there no other name under heaven by which we must be saved? Why is there only one mediator between God and men, the man Jesus Christ, the righteous? Christ Jesus is the one who gave Himself for sinners on the cross and He is the one who lives eternally to make intercession for us:

> Therefore He is also able to save to the uttermost those who come to God through Him, since He always lives to make intercession for them. (Hebrews 7:25)

> For Christ has not entered the holy places made with hands, which are copies of the true, but into heaven itself, now to appear in the presence of God for us. (Hebrews 9:24)

Christ is the only one who truly ascended — arose by His own power from earth to Heaven ("No one has ascended to heaven but He who came down from heaven, *that is,* the Son of Man who is in heaven." John 3:13), where He intercedes on our behalf. He, as God in the flesh, is omnipotent, omniscient, and omnipresent; so if you call upon Him at any time or from anywhere, He can hear you and He can help you:

> For in that He Himself has suffered, being tempted, He is able to aid those who are tempted. (Hebrews 2:18)

Christ knows all of our situations, while a human person is limited in his presence, his power, his ability, and his knowledge before and after death. Even saints[13] have a human nature that is limited in all these ways. Do we have faith enough in Christ to depend on Him alone, realizing that we have no spiritual need for anyone except Jesus? If not, let us ask the Lord to give us this faith. Remember,

Without faith it is impossible to please Him.
(Hebrews 11:6)

---

13 Saints, in Biblical terms, are all those thousands who fear, love, praise, and walk with God [EDITOR]. See more on the Biblical definition of "saints," pp. 85–88, and Lexicon, p. 138.

CHAPTER NINE

Titles Given to Blessed Mary

BLESSED MARY CALLED THE QUEEN[14]

*C*AN we call blessed Mary the Queen who is at the right hand of the King? Has she been given this title because some have read in Psalm 45:9 that, "Kings' daughters are among Your honorable women; At Your right hand stands the queen in gold from Ophir"?

Is that why we have her picture in icons on the right side of Jesus, and we call her "Our Lady" or "Queen"? Who has given Mary the right to sit on the right side of Jesus? To sit on the right or the left side of Jesus is for those God has prepared to sit there as Jesus told His disciples:

> Then the mother of Zebedee's sons came to Him with her sons, kneeling down and asking something from Him. And He said to her,

---

14 ElMasry, 47.

"What do you wish?" She said to Him, "Grant that these two sons of mine may sit, one on Your right hand and the other on the left, in Your kingdom." But Jesus answered and said, "You do not know what you ask. Are you able to drink the cup that I am about to drink, and be baptized with the baptism that I am baptized with?" They said to Him, "We are able." So He said to them, "You will indeed drink My cup, and be baptized with the baptism that I am baptized with; but to sit on My right hand and on My left is not Mine to give, but it is for those for whom it is prepared by My Father." (Matthew 20:20–23)

Christ did not say to the sons of Zebedee that He reserved sitting on His right side for His mother, Mary. He said that sitting on My right or left is not up to Me, it is for those prepared by My Father. If Mary were sitting there, the Scriptures would have mentioned her in at least one of the many places in the Word of God where it is recorded that God and His Son (the Messiah/the Lamb) sit on the throne of God in Heaven.

Let us look at a few verses which refer to Jesus sitting at the right hand of God:

The LORD said to my Lord, "Sit at My right

hand, till I make Your enemies Your footstool." (Psalm 110:1)

But this Man, after He had offered one sacrifice for sins forever, sat down at the right hand of God, from that time waiting till His enemies are made His footstool. (Hebrews 10:12–13)

God, who at various times and in various ways spoke in time past to the fathers by the prophets, has in these last days spoken to us by His Son, whom He has appointed heir of all things, through whom also He made the worlds; who being the brightness of His glory and the express image of His person, and upholding all things by the word of His power, when He had by Himself purged our sins, sat down at the right hand of the Majesty on high. (Hebrews 1:1–3)

Jesus did not accept the sincere desire of the mother of Zebedee's sons to see them honored by sitting next to Christ; and the Lord's followers are warned (Deuteronomy 4:1-2; Revelation 22:18) not to add anything to the Lord's WORDS — even if the motive is to give honor to such a wonderful, saintly woman as Mary. We cannot call her Our Master, Lady, or Queen because the Lord Jesus Christ has the Biblical title of the King of Kings and the Lord of Lords! He is the Master and King over all, including His mother Mary.

BLESSED MARY CALLED

THE LADDER OF JACOB[15]

Mary is called by some "the ladder of Jacob," referring to the ladder seen between earth and heaven in Jacob's dream:

> Then he dreamed, and behold, a ladder was set up on the earth, and its top reached to heaven; and there the angels of God were ascending and descending on it. (Genesis 28:12)

The belief is that her role in giving birth to Jesus symbolizes a ladder since she made a connection between earth and heaven. In contrast, these are Jesus' comments about the symbolism of Jacob's ladder:

> And He said to him, "Most assuredly, I say to you, hereafter you shall see heaven open, and the angels of God ascending and descending upon the Son of Man." (John 1:51)

Jesus' interpretation was that the ladder from heaven was related to His role in bringing salvation from God down to man and in preparing man to live with God in heaven. Jesus Christ, God in the flesh, is the only one

---

15 Pope Shenuda of Alexandria, article in Arabic in *Mar Yohana*—Coptic Orthodox magazine, published in Covina, CA, July 2005.

uniquely prepared by the Father and qualified to connect heaven with earth.

> He said to them, "…I came forth from the Father and have come into the world. Again, I leave the world and go to the Father." (John 16:28)

> Jesus answered him, "…In My Father's house are many mansions; if it were not so, I would have told you. I go to prepare a place for you…. I will come again and receive you to Myself; that where I am, there you may be also." (John 14:2–3)

> But now in Christ Jesus you who once were far off have been brought near by the blood of Christ. (Ephesians 2:13)

BLESSED MARY CALLED
THE BRIDE[16]

Some call Mary the true bride of the Lord of Glory referred to in the Psalms:

> Listen, O daughter, consider and incline your ear; forget your own people also, and your father's house; So the King will greatly desire your beauty; because He is your Lord, worship Him. (Psalm 45:10–11)

---

16 Pope Shenuda.

They say further that she was called the Bride in Solomon's writings or the virgin mentioned in the Song of Solomon. Mary the mother of Jesus is not the bride of Jesus. How can the mother become a bride to her own son?

These various references to a bride in the Old Testament pale in the light of the New Testament's clear teaching about the Bride of Christ. The true bride is cleansed by the Word of God and sanctified by Christ as a glorified church without spot or blemish, prepared for her Lord:

> Christ also loved the church and gave Himself for it, that He might sanctify and cleanse it with the washing of water by the word, that He might present it to Himself a glorious church, not having spot or wrinkle or any such thing, but that it should be holy and without blemish. (Ephesians 5:25–27)

The true bride of Christ is the precious church made up of those who have received Christ as Savior and are living for Him. The Scriptures represent the bride as holy Jerusalem. That is what we read in John's revelation:

> Then one of the seven angels who had the seven bowls filled with the seven last plagues came to me and talked with me, saying, "Come, I will show you the bride, the Lamb's wife." And he carried me away in the Spirit to a great and high

76

mountain, and showed me the great city, the holy Jerusalem, descending out of heaven from God, having the glory of God. Her light was like a most precious stone, like a jasper stone, clear as crystal. (Revelation 21:9–11)

This bride is to be presented to Christ at His second coming:

And I heard, as it were, the voice of a great multitude, as the sound of many waters and as the sound of mighty thunderings, saying, "Alleluia! For the Lord God Omnipotent reigns! Let us be glad and rejoice and give Him glory, for the marriage of the Lamb has come, and His wife has made herself ready." And to her it was granted to be arrayed in fine linen, clean and bright, for the fine linen is the righteous acts of the saints. (Revelation 19:6–8)

Blessed Mary called
The Beautiful Dove[17]

Some describe Mary as a beautiful dove, recalling the beautiful dove that brought to Noah an olive branch representing peace and the hope of salvation from the flood:

Then the dove came to him in the evening, and behold, a freshly plucked olive leaf was in her

---

17 Pope Shenuda.

mouth; and Noah knew that the waters had receded from the earth. (Genesis 8:11)

That is why the priest offers incense to the icon of Mary as he leaves the church and says, "Peace to you, virgin Mary, the beautiful dove." Our comment is that this practice is an offense to the truth of God's Word that commands us not to bow down, venerate, or serve any graven image or likeness of anything that is in heaven or earth or in the water (Exodus 20:4–5).

Listen to the seriousness of the Lord's words that Moses spoke to the people of Israel:

> Take careful heed to yourselves, for you saw no form when the LORD spoke to you at Horeb out of the midst of the fire, lest you act corruptly and make for yourselves a carved image in the form of any figure: the likeness of male or female, the likeness of any animal that is on the earth or the likeness of any winged bird that flies in the air, the likeness of anything that creeps on the ground or the likeness of any fish that is in the water beneath the earth.
>
> And take heed, lest you lift your eyes to heaven, and when you see the sun, the moon, and the stars, all the host of heaven, you feel driven to worship them and serve them, which

the LORD your God has given to all the peoples under the whole heaven as a heritage.

Take heed to yourselves, lest you forget the covenant of the LORD your God which He made with you, and make for yourselves a carved image in the form of anything which the LORD your God has forbidden you. For the LORD your God is a consuming fire, a jealous God.

(Deuteronomy 4:15–19, 23–24)

BLESSED MARY CALLED
THE MOTHER OF GOD[18]

As we have mentioned earlier, this title given the mother of Jesus was a big mistake growing out of the Council of Ephesus (held in A.D. 431) in which Mary was called "the mother of our Lord." This second title is Biblical in that Mary is the mother of our Lord Jesus Christ. The Bible uses the term *Lord* to refer to God, to the Messiah, and to an honorable human who is in authority.

Let us go further in expanding on what we discussed at the end of Chapter One. In the greeting from Mary's cousin, Elizabeth (Luke 1:43), the word translated "mother" (*waledah*) in the Arabic language literally means "the one who gives birth to a child" (*walad*); and there is no doubt

18 ElMasry, 49, and Noll and Fallon, 206.

79

that Mary was truly the human vessel that gave birth to Jesus Christ, our Lord.

God prepared and used the blessed Mary as the vessel to house and nurture the infant Jesus. However, while Jesus Christ was 100 percent human, He was also *uniquely* at the same time 100 percent Divine and the One who had created Mary (John 1:3).

The error comes when Mary is thought to be the mother of either God the Father who is a Spirit (John 4:24) present from eternity, or the mother of God the Son, the pre-existent second person of the Triune God. No one was present with the Triune God in the beginning; He had no mother or father. Moses said in his prayer,

> Lord, You have been our dwelling place in all generations. Before the mountains were brought forth, or ever You had formed the earth and the world, even from everlasting to everlasting, You are God. (Psalm 90:1–2)

The first time we knew of God was at the time of creation:

> In the beginning God created the heavens and the earth. (Genesis 1:1)

> Then God said, "Let Us make man in Our image, according to Our likeness;..." So God

created man in His own image; in the image
of God He created him; male and female He
created them. (Genesis 1:26–27)

The Mother of God error has also opened the door to
the misunderstanding and false teaching by other religions
and cults that Mary and God the Father had sexual relations, which is a complete blasphemy!

The Apostle John who was given the revelation from God
about the WORD OF GOD's (Jesus Christ's) pre-incarnation
role in creation (John 1:1–3), and knew Mary better than
any other New Testament writer, except James, never mentions her role in the physical birth of Christ at all. All he
says is that,

> The Word became flesh and dwelt among us.
> (John 1:14)

BLESSED MARY CALLED
THE DOOR[19]

We know that Christ is the door, not Mary. Jesus calls
Himself the entryway to life and salvation in John 14:6:

> Jesus said to him, "I am the way, the truth, and
> the life. No one comes to the Father except
> through Me."

---

19 Pope Shenuda.

Christ's own words deny any other door than Himself:

> Jesus said unto them again, ... "I am the door.
> If anyone enters by Me, he will be saved, and
> will go in and out and find pasture." (John 10:9)

Peter said the same thing in Acts:

> Nor is there salvation in any other, for there is
> no other name under heaven given among men
> by which we must be saved. (4:12)

Some people say that the church is the door because of what Jacob said about the place of his dream at Bethel:

> And he was afraid and said, "How awesome is
> this place! This is none other than the house
> of God, and this is the gate of heaven!"
>
> (Genesis 28:17)

Jacob, in referring to the house of God as the door of heaven, referred to the location in which he experienced his strange dream. In this dream, God spoke to him personally, promising that all people on earth would be blessed through him and his offspring.

The church is not the door to heaven. The church is the people whom God is bringing together to build a dwelling place for Himself.

For we are God's fellow workers; you are God's
field; you are God's building.

(1 Corinthians 3:9)

Blessed Mary called
The Holy of Holies[20]

The Holy of Holies was the part of the temple in which
the chief priest entered once a year to offer sacrifices for all
the people; while the virgin Mary was the one the Lord of
Glory entered by the Holy Spirit once to prepare the body
of the One who would redeem the whole world.

At the time that Jesus was in the virgin Mary's womb,
He was a small fetus. It was at the time of His death that
He became the Chief Priest, who entered into heaven (the
true Holy of Holies) itself:

> For Christ has not entered the holy places made
> with hands, which are copies of the true, but into
> heaven itself, now to appear in the presence of
> God for us; not that He should offer Himself
> often, as the high priest enters the Most Holy
> Place every year with blood of another—He
> then would have had to suffer often since the
> foundation of the world; but now, once at the
> end of the ages, He has appeared to put away sin
> by the sacrifice of Himself. (Hebrews 9:24–26)

---

20 Pope Shenuda.

> But Christ came as High Priest of the good
> things to come, with the greater and more perfect
> tabernacle not made with hands, that is, not of
> this creation. Not with the blood of goats and
> calves, but with His own blood He entered the
> Most Holy Place once for all, having obtained
> eternal redemption. (Hebrews 9:11–12)

There is nothing in the Scriptures to denote that any person could be the location or the place where the blood sacrifice made atonement for sin (the Holy of Holies); and the Word of God does not apply such a title to Mary. Blessed Mary was a human being, she died as a human being, and she continued being a human being after she died.

Christ has already completed the High Priestly work with His own sacrifice. Therefore, it is unnecessary to attempt mediation through Mary to God. More importantly, it is an act of disbelief in the sufficiency of salvation through the Son of God. Look at God's words:

> Thus says the LORD: "Cursed is the man who
> trusts in man and makes flesh his strength, whose
> heart departs from the LORD. For he shall be like
> a shrub in the desert, and shall not see when good
> comes, but shall inhabit the parched places in the
> wilderness, in a salt land which is not inhabited.
> "Blessed is the man who trusts in the LORD,

and whose hope is the LORD. For he shall be like a tree planted by the waters, which spreads out its roots by the river, and will not fear when heat comes; but its leaf will be green, and will not be anxious in the year of drought, nor will cease from yielding fruit." (Jeremiah 17:5–8)

The objective of the church and its ministers is to help people to know the truth and to depend completely on Him:

It is better to trust in the LORD than to put confidence in man. (Psalm 118:8)

Do not put your trust in princes, nor in a son of man, in whom there is no help. His spirit departs, he returns to his earth; in that very day his plans perish. (Psalm 146:3–4)

CAN WE CALL HER SAINT MARY?

Yes, but we must realize the designation of *saint* belongs not just to blessed Mary, but to every believer, man or woman, who believes from the heart in Christ crucified and resurrected. Let us see how Jesus considers us believers through the writing of Paul:

It is because of Him that you are in Christ Jesus, who has become for us wisdom from God—that

is, our righteousness, holiness, and redemption.
(1 Corinthians 1:30, NIV)

Therefore, Christ is our sanctification. All whom He redeems and live *in Him* become *saints*. God gives this title to every believer. We require no decree from any church leader or leaders, those who would presume to give that title to whomever they wish. Paul used this title for *all* believers and we can see this in his epistles:

> To all who are in Rome, beloved of God, called to be saints. (Romans 1:7)

> Paul, called to be an apostle of Jesus Christ through the will of God, and Sosthenes our brother, To the church of God which is at Corinth, to those who are sanctified in Christ Jesus, called to be saints, with all who in every place call on the name of Jesus Christ our Lord, both theirs and ours. (1 Corinthians 1:1–2)

> Paul, an apostle of Jesus Christ by the will of God, and Timothy our brother, To the church of God which is at Corinth, with all the saints who are in all Achaia. (2 Corinthians 1:1)

> Paul, an apostle of Jesus Christ by the will of God, To the saints who are in Ephesus, and faithful in Christ Jesus. (Ephesians 1:1)

Paul and Timothy, bond-servants of Christ
Jesus, to all the saints in Christ Jesus who are
in Philippi, including the overseers and deacons.
(Philippians 1:1, NASB)

Paul, an apostle of Jesus Christ by the will of
God, and Timothy our brother, to the saints and
faithful brethren in Christ who are in Colosse:
(Colossians 1:1–2, NASB)

From all those verses—which are as clear as the light
from the sun—we see that the Lord gives the title "saint" to
every true believer and not just to Mary. No doubt, blessed
Mary is a saint and we can call her that, but that title also
belongs to all believers in Jesus Christ who experience Him.
It is not the right of any human being to give this title to
only a certain few Christians brought to His attention; this
is contrary to the teachings of the Word of God.

The Scriptures have the answer for this whole dilemma
that resulted from the attribution of undeserved titles for
blessed Mary in order to elevate faith in her identity, position, and power:

Trust in the LORD with all your heart, and lean
not on your own understanding. In all your
ways acknowledge Him, and He shall direct
your paths. (Proverbs 3:5–6)

Oh, taste and see that the LORD is good; blessed is the man who trusts in Him! (Psalm 34:8)

You will keep him in perfect peace, whose mind is stayed on You, because he trusts in You. Trust in the LORD forever, for in YAH, the LORD, is everlasting strength. (Isaiah 26:3–4)

Chapter Ten

Prayers to Blessed Mary

*T*HOSE in the traditional churches pray to blessed Mary, calling her "the Mother of Light," requesting her to ask the Lord to give salvation to the world and help people against temptations.

They call her "the Mother of Light"[21] to whom incense must be offered; while we know it is to the Lord only that incense should be offered:

> "For from the rising of the sun, even to its going down, My name shall be great among the Gentiles; in every place incense shall be offered to My name, and a pure offering; for My name shall be great among the nations," says the LORD of hosts. (Malachi 1:11)

Another prayer says, "O Mother of God you are the

---

21 ElMasry, 49.

true vine that carries the grape [fruit] of life;"[22] and yet we know that it is Jesus who is the true vine.

> Jesus...said to him,..."I am the true vine, and My Father is the vinedresser." (John 15:1)

A third prayer asks Mary to mediate on our behalf to the Son who was born to her; because of her purity, the Lord will accept her mediation. Some prayers ask her not to reject us, evil ones, from her mediation. Another prayer calls upon her saying, "Oh, pure Virgin, come down and give us your support; remove bad thoughts from us. You are the merciful mother of the origin of life, my king and Lord Jesus Christ; you are the protector of our salvation, and you are the one who will never reject our pleas to you."

In another prayer, Mary is called "the Beautiful Flower" that is unchangeable.[23] God's Word says that God is the one who never changes. It is clear that only God and no human, including Mary, can be called *unchangeable*:

> For I *am* the LORD, I do not change. (Malachi 3:6)

> Every good gift and every perfect gift is from above, and comes down from the Father of lights, with whom there is no variation or shadow of turning. (James 1:17)

---

22 *El Ajbiah*, Arabic language prayer book (Cairo, Egypt: Coptic Orthodox Church).
23 *El Ajbiah*.

Another prayer says that we have no excuse for our sins and we know that our Lord will only accept Mary's mediation.[24] This implies that Mary has more kindness and mercy toward us than Jesus does, while we know that the love of Jesus is much bigger and higher than that of anyone else, including Mary:

> Now before the Feast of the Passover, when Jesus knew that His hour had come that He should depart from this world to the Father, having loved His own who were in the world, He loved them to the end. (John 13:1)

While the Scripture writers never mention anything about the love of blessed Mary for us, they are full of words commending the love of Christ. After having had his personal revelation and experience with the Lord, the Apostle Paul makes the intensity of Christ's love very clear:

> For the love of Christ compels us, because we judge thus: that if One died for all, then all died. (2 Corinthians 5:14)

> I have been crucified with Christ; it is no longer I who live, but Christ lives in me; and the life which I now live in the flesh I live by faith in

---

24 *El Ajbiah.*

the Son of God, who loved me and gave Himself for me. (Galatians 2:20)

That Christ may dwell in your hearts through faith; that you, being rooted and grounded in love, may be able to comprehend with all the saints what is the width and length and depth and height—to know the love of Christ which passes knowledge; that you may be filled with all the fullness of God. (Ephesians 3:17–19)

Jesus, Himself, expressed His love for His followers many times:

Jesus said, "A new commandment I give to you, that you love one another; as I have loved you, that you also love one another." (John 13:34)

"He who has My commandments and keeps them, it is he who loves Me. And he who loves Me will be loved by My Father, and I will love him and manifest Myself to him." (John 14:21)

"As the Father loved Me, I also have loved you; abide in My love. If you keep My commandments, you will abide in My love, just as I have kept My Father's commandments and abide in His love.... This is My commandment, that you love one another as I have loved you. Greater love has no one than this, than to lay down one's life for his friends." (John 15:9–10, 12–13)

And I have declared to them Your name, and will declare it, that the love with which You loved Me may be in them, and I in them. (John 17:26)

The other thing very clear in the Word of God is that the true believer has the right and obligation to go directly to the throne of grace:

Seeing then that we have a great High Priest who has passed through the heavens, Jesus the Son of God, let us hold fast our confession. For we do not have a High Priest who cannot sympathize with our weaknesses, but was in all points tempted as we are, yet without sin. Let us therefore come boldly to the throne of grace, that we may obtain mercy and find grace to help in time of need. (Hebrews 4:14–16)

Therefore, those who are born anew from above (John 3:3), do not need to go through any other person to get to God; the only personal Redeemer and Mediator is Jesus Christ.

In another of the prayers of the traditional churches, the praying persons say, "O Mother of God, your perfect mediation casts away all our fear; your strong support will protect us."[25] This portrays Mary as a trustworthy object of faith, the source of goodness and help, and the powerful guardian who protects those who call upon her. This means that they are attributing to her the power of God, but the Bible teaches that we are to trust only in the Lord:

> In the fear of the LORD there is strong confidence, and His children will have a place of refuge. (Proverbs 14:26)

> I will lift up my eyes to the hills—from whence comes my help? My help comes from the Lord, who made heaven and earth. (Psalm 121:1–2)

The only armor for the believer is the Lord:

> Our soul waits for the LORD; He is our help and our shield. (Psalm 33:20)

> After these things the word of the LORD came to Abram in a vision, saying, "Do not be afraid, Abram. I am your shield, your exceedingly great reward." (Genesis 15:1)

> As for God, His way is perfect; the word of the LORD is proven; He is a shield to all who trust in Him. (Psalm 18:30)

---

25 *El Ajbiah.*

But You, O LORD, are a shield for me, my glory
and the One who lifts up my head. (Psalm 3:3)

Therefore, nobody who has already tasted the Lord and experienced His salvation has any reason to go back and put his trust in any human person, including blessed Mary.

In one of their prayers, those who pray to Mary call her "Hedge of our Salvation."[26] In contrast, Zechariah 2:5 says the Lord is our hedge:

"For I," says the LORD, "will be a wall of fire all
around her, and I will be the glory in her midst."

Some pray saying, "You are the one who makes void the counsel of the ungodly and exchanges the sadness of your slaves to joy because you are our hope, O Mother of God."[27] With all of these descriptions referring to their faith in Mary, what do they leave for God?

From the Bible we learn just the opposite — God is the only hope for the believers:

And now, Lord, what do I wait for? (Psalm 39:7)

Why are you cast down, O my soul? And why
are you disquieted within me? Hope in God;
for I shall yet praise Him, the help of my coun-
tenance and my God. (Psalm 42:11)

---

26 *El Ajbiah.*
27 *El Ajbiah.*

The full salvation we receive in Christ satisfies all our hopes and dreams, even the desires of our hearts. Those who have received it have no need to place their hope in anyone else, including blessed Mary:

> Blessed be the God and Father of our Lord Jesus Christ, who according to His abundant mercy has begotten us again to a living hope through the resurrection of Jesus Christ from the dead, to an inheritance incorruptible and undefiled and that does not fade away, reserved in heaven for you, who are kept by the power of God through faith for salvation ready to be revealed in the last time. (1 Peter 1:3–5)

God is the only one who can change our sadness into joy, and those who pray to Mary asking her to do that for them, calling themselves her "slaves," do not understand the teaching of the Word of God. Christ has liberated true believers from slavery to Satan and sin (Romans 6:17–20). Christ became incarnate for this very purpose. These are the words of the prophet Isaiah about the Lord Jesus:

> The Spirit of the Lord GOD *is* upon Me, because the LORD has anointed Me to preach good tidings to the poor; He has sent Me to heal the brokenhearted, to proclaim liberty to the captives,

and the opening of the prison to those who are bound. (Isaiah 61:1)

Jesus quoted these words in the synagogue and,

> Then He closed the book, and gave it back to the attendant and sat down. And the eyes of all who were in the synagogue were fixed on Him. And He began to say to them, "Today this Scripture is fulfilled in your hearing." (Luke 4:20–21)

Those liberated by Christ have become servants of the Lord (Romans 1:1; 6:22); they are not slaves of Mary. The Lord Jesus taught us that He is our Master:

> One is your Teacher, the Christ, (Matthew 23:8)

and that it is impossible to serve more than one Master,

> saying, ... "No one can serve two masters; for either he will hate the one and love the other, or else he will be loyal to the one and despise the other." (Matthew 6:24)

In another of their prayers, the blessed Mary is called "The Door of Human Intelligence."[28] From where would Mary find the power and wisdom to save from his or her difficulties anyone who comes to her by faith? How can Mary, with her spirit in heaven and her body in an earthly

---

28 *El Ajbiah.*

grave, save anyone from difficulties? Why would anyone forsake his faith in the Lord who is everywhere and is able to help in every situation, in order to put his faith in Mary who is so limited?

Do the angels of heaven obey Mary and act immediately to help those who have resorted to her for salvation from difficulties? This is the work of God alone.

David and all the faithful people of God in the Scriptures directed their prayers only to the Lord:

> The troubles of my heart have enlarged; bring me out of my distresses! (Psalm 25:17)

> Do not let me be ashamed, O LORD, for I have called upon You; let the wicked be ashamed; let them be silent in the grave. (Psalm 31:17)

> The righteous cry out, and the LORD hears, and delivers them out of all their troubles. (Psalm 34:17)

> Then they cried out to the LORD in their trouble, and He delivered them out of their distresses. (Psalm 107:6)

> Then they cried out to the LORD in their trouble, and He saved them out of their distresses. (Psalm 107:13)

> Then they cry out to the LORD in their trouble,

and He brings them out of their distresses. He
calms the storm, so that its waves are still. Then
they are glad because they are quiet; so He guides
them to their desired haven. (Psalm 107:28–30)

There is no need to pray to Mary. Can she go to those
who are in distress in ships on the sea in order to calm the
storms and save them? Faith must be in the Lord alone:

Without faith it is impossible to please Him,
for he who comes to God must believe that
He is, and that He is a rewarder of those who
diligently seek Him. (Hebrews 11:6)

In another of these types of baseless prayers, some pray,
"Have mercy on us, O Lord. Your mercy comes by the
mediation of the greatest mediator; the origin of purity,
goodness, and blessings" (referring to Mary).[29]

The beloved disciple John assures us with the words of
God that our mediator is Jesus Christ, the righteous, and
no other:

If anyone sins, we have an Advocate with the
Father, Jesus Christ the righteous. (1 John 2:1)

The only true kinds of human prayers interceding on
behalf of others to God are those made by believers here

---

29 *El Ajbiah.*

who are still alive. Abraham was able to intercede in prayer for the city of Sodom because he was alive here on earth at that time.

Saints who are now dead cannot appeal or pray on behalf of anyone; death does not turn them into gods. The God-Man Jesus Christ is the only one always living and available eternally everywhere; and His power is above and beyond us all:

> Therefore He [Christ] is also able to save to the uttermost those who come to God through Him, since He always lives to make intercession for them. (Hebrews 7:25)

The act of making petitions by praying to Mary is contrary to the Lord Jesus Christ's words and deserves this warning:

> If anyone teaches otherwise and does not consent to wholesome words, even the words of our Lord Jesus Christ, and to the doctrine which accords with godliness, he is proud, knowing nothing, but is obsessed with disputes and arguments over words, from which come envy, strife, reviling, evil suspicions, useless wranglings of men of corrupt minds and destitute of the truth, who suppose that godliness is a means of gain. From such withdraw yourself. (1 Timothy 6:3–5)

CHAPTER ELEVEN

Rumored Appearances of Blessed Mary

*L*ET us remind you of a story which the Lord told about a rich man and a poor man named Lazarus in Luke 16:19–31. I believe, as other commentators do, that this is a true story and not just a parable because Jesus mentioned Abraham and Lazarus, which were names of actual people.[30]

Jesus said that in the afterlife, the rich man after dying and going to Hell, asked Abraham, whom Lazarus was with in Heaven, to have mercy on him, and asked him to send Lazarus with a drop of water on the tip of his finger to cool his tongue. But Abraham replied that "there is a great gulf fixed, so that those who want to pass from here to you cannot" (Luke 16:26), that it is not possible to pass between Hell and Heaven.

---

30 Calvin prefers to think of this as a *true* story; however, he nonetheless emphasizes rather the truth of the lesson—John Calvin *Commentary on a Harmony of the Evangelists, Matthew, Mark, and Luke*, Volume I (Grand Rapids: Baker Book House, 1996), 184.

The rich man then asked Abraham to send Lazarus back to the land of the living to give testimony to his five brothers who were still alive so that they would not also end up in that place of torment. Abraham's answer was definite: the brothers already "have Moses and the prophets; let them hear them" (Luke 16:29). They have all the recorded Scriptures so that they can read and then repent.

The only way to *true* repentance is by hearing the Word of God and following it:

> Seek the LORD while He may be found, call upon Him while He is near. Let the wicked forsake his way, and the unrighteous man his thoughts; let him return to the LORD, and He will have mercy on him; and to our God, for He will abundantly pardon. (Isaiah 55:6–7)

Let them also listen to the words of Hosea the prophet:

> Take words with you and return to the LORD. Say to Him: "Forgive all our sins and receive us graciously, that we may offer the fruit of our lips." (Hosea 14:2, NIV)

Therefore, if a man does not listen and heed the testimony of the Word of God that is pure, he is already lost, sinking in ignorance (including even the "sacred heresies" he has been taught).

The Lord Jesus Christ speaking to the Jews,

> Said to them, "He who is of God hears God's words; therefore you do not hear, because you are not of God." (John 8:47)

The only basis and reference by which we draw closer to God is the Holy Bible. The secret behind the decline of true faith that has taken place in the nominal Christian church is a result of neglecting and putting aside the Word of God, and following, instead, the traditions of men.

Jesus concluded Abraham's conversation with the rich man by saying,

> But he said to him, "If they do not hear Moses and the prophets, neither will they be persuaded though one rise from the dead." (Luke 16:31)

Lazarus could not give testimony to the brothers of the rich man because he could not rise up from the dead. He could not put on a body and go to the brothers because without resurrection it is impossible for the spirits of the dead to connect with the earth. According to that same Biblical truth, Mary would come *not* back and reveal herself to anyone.

The only one who is able to return bodily and show Himself to anybody is Jesus Christ. He does reveal Himself when the Holy Spirit enlightens our understanding of the words recorded in the Bible, when He calls someone to follow and serve Him, and He lovingly reveals Himself to those who love and obey Him:

> Jesus said…, "He who has My commandments and keeps them, it is he who loves Me. And he who loves Me will be loved by My Father, and I will love him and manifest Myself to him. (John 14:21)

The Lord Jesus Christ showed Himself to Saul of Tarsus (later called the Apostle Paul) in order to change his heart, to change his direction, and to remove his blind fanaticism. He sent Ananias to lay hands on him and tell him:

> Brother Saul, the Lord Jesus, who appeared to you on the road as you came, has sent me that you may receive your sight and be filled with the Holy Spirit. (Acts 9:17)

When the Lord showed himself to Saul, He spoke to him in his Hebrew language,

> And He said, "…But rise and stand on your feet; for I have appeared to you for this purpose, to make you a minister and a witness both of the things which you have seen and of the things which I will yet reveal to you.

> "I will deliver you from the Jewish people, as
> well as from the Gentiles, to whom I now send
> you, to open their eyes, in order to turn them
> from darkness to light, and from the power of
> Satan to God, that they may receive forgiveness
> of sins and an inheritance among those who are
> sanctified by faith in Me." (Acts 26:16–18)

When Jesus showed Himself to Paul, He spoke and
Paul was able to hear His voice and understand His words;
but did Mary ever speak to any of those people who
claim she appeared to them? If so, what *language* did she
speak? Did anyone else hear the voice of Mary? Did she
give a message to anybody? If so, what was the message?
Certainly, the Scriptures never recorded any appearance
of Mary the mother of Jesus after her death. Who from
among us living today has seen Mary when she was alive
on earth, so that we could say for sure that the picture on
top of the church (or wherever) was certainly a true image
of the blessed Mary?

Some say that they have seen blessed Mary carrying
the baby, Jesus. This is very strange. We know that Jesus
died on the cross when He was 33 years old. Does that
mean that Jesus Christ came back again as a baby and His
mother now carries Him about? Certainly, this cannot be
so. In addition, the Lord God has strictly forbidden having
mediums and contact with the spirits of the dead.

We read in Deuteronomy:

> When you come into the land which the LORD
> your God is giving you, you shall not learn to
> follow the abominations of those nations. There
> shall not be found among you anyone who makes
> his son or his daughter pass through the fire, or
> one who practices witchcraft, or a soothsayer, or
> one who interprets omens, or a sorcerer, or one
> who conjures spells, or a medium, or a spiritist,
> or one who calls up the dead. For all who do
> these things are an abomination to the LORD,
> and because of these abominations the LORD your
> God drives them out from before you. (18:9–12)

Therefore, for the church to teach connection with the
dead, no matter how holy these persons were, is a heresy,
and whoever tries to make connection with the dead is
not accepted and will even be punished by the Lord. The
Scriptures give no exception.

We understand from the teachings of the Bible that the
spirit of Saint Mary is now in Paradise with all the true
believers in God, and she will continue to be there until
the Lord returns and gives her a glorified body. It is only
then she will appear—together with the other saints.

Concerning the physical body of Mary, we know that it
is somewhere in an unknown grave in Palestine, in a place

that the Lord did not mention in the New Testament. The physical body of blessed Mary is not in heaven. If the body of Mary were in heaven after her death, the New Testament would have mentioned that as it mentioned Elijah's bodily assumption to heaven in 2 Kings 2:11–12.

On November 27, 2005, the Associated Press reported that Christians were gathering to see the tears of blessed Mary emanating from a statue of her likeness. Huge numbers of Catholics in Sacramento, California, were gathered with rosaries in hand along with cameras to see the statue in the Vietnamese Catholic Martyrs' Church. Many people reported that they saw tears, colored like blood, falling from her eyes. They say that these tears were a miracle. The news story suggested that appearances of blessed Mary motivate people to talk about the human spirit.

There is no doubt that Mary was human and her spirit is a human spirit. But what does the Bible say about the human spirit? Let us see what the Bible says about its nature and destiny.

• THE FIRST TRUTH is that the Lord is the one who gives the spirit to man, and this spirit dwells inside the man:

> The burden of the word of the LORD against Israel. Thus says the LORD, who stretches out the heavens, lays the foundation of the earth, and forms the spirit of man within him. (Zechariah 12:1)

Let the LORD, the God of the spirits of all flesh,
set a man over the congregation. (Numbers 27:16)

Furthermore, we have had human fathers who
corrected us, and we paid them respect. Shall
we not much more readily be in subjection to
the Father of spirits and live? (Hebrews 12:9)

All the ways of a man are pure in his own eyes,
but the LORD weighs the spirits. (Proverbs 16:2)

• THE SECOND TRUTH is that the spirit given by God is
the secret of life inside the body.

For as the body without the spirit is dead, so
faith without works is dead also. (James 2:26)

Do not put your trust in princes, nor in a son
of man, in whom there is no help. His spirit
departs, he returns to his earth; in that very day
his plans perish. (Psalm 146:3–4)

Then the dust will return to the earth as it was,
and the spirit will return to God who gave it.
(Ecclesiastes 12:7)

• THE THIRD TRUTH is that the spirit given to human beings
is the center of spiritual worship. The Apostle Paul said:

For God is my witness, whom I serve *with my*

spirit in the gospel of His Son, that without ceasing I make mention of you always in my prayers. (Romans 1:9, *emphasis added*.)

David, worshipping in the Spirit, wrote:

To the end that my glory may sing praise to You and not be silent. O LORD my God, I will give thanks to You forever. (Psalm 30:12)

Jesus said to the Samaritan woman:

God is Spirit, and those who worship Him must worship in spirit and truth. (John 4:24)

• THE FOURTH TRUTH is that this spirit cannot connect with people on earth after leaving the body; this applies to all human beings whom the Triune God (Father, Son, and Holy Spirit) created, including blessed Mary:

For when a few years are finished, I shall go the way of no return. (Job 16:22)

For the living know that they will die; but the dead know nothing, and they have no more reward, for the memory of them is forgotten. Also their love, their hatred, and their envy have now perished; nevermore will they have a share in anything done under the sun. (Ecclesiastes 9:5–6)

Therefore, the dead person's relationship with everything under the sun is gone; it is finished.

As we have mentioned before, in Chapter Seven, the Apostle Paul's words in Philippians 1:21–22 are like a beacon of light. Paul declares that while death would release him from the pains and suffering connected with his earthly body, death would also prevent him from serving the brothers in Philippi. If Paul were to live, his continuation in the flesh would make it possible for him to continue serving them, but death would make that impossible.

If after leaving the body the human spirit were able to connect with people on earth, Paul would have told the brothers that he would come back in his spirit to support them and strengthen their faith. If there had been the possibility that Paul might reappear to his fellow believers and/or to serve them after death, he would certainly have encouraged and comforted them by telling them so.

It is very clear that death forbids humans, no matter how holy were their characters or how important their spiritual service, to continue their earthy functions.

> Also there were many priests, because they were prevented by death from continuing. (Hebrews 7:23)

Therefore, we see that death completely terminates the earthly experiences and functions of ministers, priests, and saints, as well as every other believer, and their relationship with the earthly population is no more. Therefore, Mary (and all the other saints) died as every human being dies.

> And as it is appointed for men to die once, but after this the judgment. (Hebrews 9:27)

It is a very dangerous doctrine to believe that the spirits of the saints who died come back, appear, speak, and make miracles for the people on earth. This teaching opens the door for the evil practice of those claiming that you can communicate with all spirits, including satanic phenomena or affairs that are completely unclean and ungodly. The spirits of the demons can imitate those of humans (whether they were good or bad people), and their purpose is to confuse and lead astray the believers in God. The Scriptures tell us in 2 Corinthians 11:14 that "Satan himself transforms himself into an angel of light."

We all remember that the ungodly King Saul went to a woman who was practicing witchcraft in order to bring back Samuel the prophet from the dead to give advice as to what the king should do (1 Samuel 28:3–20). Samuel had been faithful to the Lord and had anointed Saul as king in keeping with the Lord's instruction. He had wept as he prayed for King Saul when he had revolted against the Lord and disobeyed His commandments. In the war between the Philistines and Israel, the Lord, because of

King Saul's disobedience, did not guide him by the godly methods (such as dreams and words from the prophets) used at that time.

Saul did not repent or humble himself to the Lord, but went instead to the demonic powers of magic in order to get for himself the Prophet Samuel's guidance. To consult with the dead is an old sin that has been among the pagan peoples, but here we see that it had entered Israel.

The incident of bringing the Prophet Samuel's spirit back has caused a lot of controversy among Bible interpreters; but this is not the place to discuss these different interpretations. What we must focus on in this subject of attempting to communicate with the spirits of the dead is the tremendous anger of the Lord toward King Saul for trying to do this. This is what we learn:

1. The spirit of the Prophet Samuel did not come back on his own, but came because of a sorcerer using magic. This should cause us to think.

2. When the Prophet Samuel came, he was not apparent to all who were in the room, not even to King Saul. Only the sorcerer saw him. She described him as an old man covered with a mantle; and Saul is the one who identified him as Samuel from her description.

3. When the spirit of the Prophet Samuel spoke to King Saul, he asked, "Why did you bother me by bringing

me back?" This means that Samuel had been in a place of rest, and bringing back him to Saul was disturbing to him. In His sovereignty, God allowed the appearance of Samuel from the dead in that event under His permissive will.

4. The Prophet Samuel reminded Saul of all his sins and disobedience against the commandments of God and informed him of the punishment coming upon him. What was the Lord's punishment coming upon a king who tried to communicate with a dead saint? We find this answer in 1 Chronicles:

> So Saul died for his unfaithfulness which he had committed against the LORD, because he did not keep the word of the LORD, and also because he consulted a medium for guidance. But he did not inquire of the LORD; therefore He killed him, and turned the kingdom over to David the son of Jesse. (10:13–14)

Let us answer this question: After seeing this example in the Word of God, should we try to connect with the spirits of the dead?

The accounts of Mary's appearances are so surprising that we must ask, why does blessed Mary appear but not Christ? Why not the Apostle Paul or the Apostle Peter, both of whom died as martyrs; or why not John the disciple whom Jesus loved so much? Why is the claim always that blessed Mary appears?

History tells us about the practice of worshipping women, especially in the old pagan religions. In their ancient religion, the Egyptians worshipped Isis the goddess of fertility and the sister and wife of Osiris. In the countries of Arabia before Islam, the Arabs worshipped the female deities called Alat, Azi, and Mnat. The Greeks worshipped Aphrodite, the goddess of love and beauty, and the Romans worshipped Venus, the goddess of love and beauty as well as Diana, the goddess of the moon and wild animals.

In Asia, the population of Ephesus worshipped Artemis the goddess of the moon who was a virgin and the sister of Apollo. Asians believed that her statue came from heaven.

> And when the city clerk had quieted the crowd, he said: "Men of Ephesus, what man is there who does not know that the city of the Ephesians is temple guardian of the great goddess Diana, and of the image which fell down from Zeus?" (Acts 19:35)

In addition, in Sidon, Lebanon, the people of that city worshipped Ashtoreth (also called Astarte), the famous goddess of sexual immorality and fertility. We note that his wives from Sidon changed the heart of Solomon to go after their gods. This shows how a person who knew the true

God of Israel and His commandments could gradually come to accept ungodly false beliefs from surrounding cultures or religions when those whom he loved introduced them.

How sad that even King Solomon, the wisest man on earth, could be seduced to worship false gods. As a result, the Lord was angry and withheld the blessings He had prepared for Solomon and his family.

Man's heart is more deceptive than anything, and any deviation from the Word of God leads one gradually into darkness:

> For it was so, when Solomon was old, that his wives turned his heart after other gods; and his heart was not loyal to the LORD his God, as was the heart of his father David. For Solomon went after Ashtoreth the goddess of the Sidonians, and after Milcom the abomination of the Ammonites. Solomon did evil in the sight of the LORD, and did not fully follow the LORD, as did his father David. Then Solomon built a high place for Chemosh the abomination of Moab, on the hill that is east of Jerusalem, and for Molech the abomination of the people of Ammon. And he did likewise for all his foreign wives, who burned incense and sacrificed to their gods.
>
> So the LORD became angry with Solomon, because his heart had turned from the LORD

God of Israel, who had appeared to him twice,
and had commanded him concerning this thing,
that he should not go after other gods; but he
did not keep what the LORD had commanded.
(1 Kings 11:4–10)

Also, at other times when the people of Israel backslid
away from the Lord their God, they worshipped the goddess called the Queen of Heaven. We read about this in the
writings of the prophet Jeremiah (7:16–18), whom God had
told not to pray for the people because the Lord had seen
their worship of the Queen of Heaven and was preparing
their punishment:

> Therefore thus says the Lord God: "Behold, My
> anger and My fury will be poured out on this
> place — on man and on beast, on the trees of
> the field and on the fruit of the ground. And it
> will burn and not be quenched." (Jeremiah 7:20)

When a remnant had escaped the Babylonian captivity
and moved to Egypt, we read again about the "Queen of
Heaven" still being worshipped by the unfaithful Israelites
(Jeremiah 44:15–19). When they refused to heed the warning of Jeremiah, the Lord Himself told them:

> Therefore hear the word of the LORD, all Judah
> who dwell in the land of Egypt: "Behold, I have

sworn by My great name," says the LORD....

"Behold, I will watch over them for adversity and not for good. And all the men of Judah...shall be consumed by the sword and by famine, until there is an end to them...."

"And this shall be a sign to you," says the LORD, "that I will punish you in this place, that you may know that My words will surely stand against you for adversity." (Jeremiah 44:26–27, 29)

All these examples show the Lord's anger against the people of Israel—those who called Him their Lord—because they offered incense to the Queen of Heaven. Should not the fear of the Lord fall upon us and anyone else who would try to elevate in their affections and show deep devotion and service to anything or anyone beside HIM?

Let us have grace, by which we may serve God acceptably with reverence and godly fear. For our God is a consuming fire. (Hebrews 12:28–29)

CHAPTER TWELVE

Miracles of Blessed Mary

*E*VERY time we hear that blessed Mary has appeared in various places, there are always rumors that she has performed miracles. Let us try to answer some questions relating to miracles and discuss this Biblically.

1. WHAT IS THE OBJECTIVE DEFINITION OF A MIRACLE?

The *Webster's New Collegiate Dictionary*, 6th Edition, defines a miracle as "an extraordinary...or abnormal event brought about by superhuman agency." It is supernatural, that is why we call it God's work.

When Jesus changed the water into wine in Cana of Galilee, it was a miracle (John 2:1–11). When He gave sight to the man born blind, it was a miracle (John 9:1–7). And when He raised Lazarus after four days of death and decay in the grave, it was a miracle (John 11:38–44). All of these were miracles because the actions are something beyond the laws of nature (supernatural) and beyond human ability.

2. How did Christ perform miracles?

We are told that,

> He cast out the spirits with a word, and healed
> all who were sick. (Matthew 8:16)

One word from the Lord Jesus Christ removed the evil spirits from the bodies they had entered. One word from Him purified the leper:

> And behold, a leper came and worshiped Him,
> saying, "Lord, if You are willing, You can make
> me clean."
> Then Jesus put out His hand and touched him,
> saying, "I am willing; be cleansed." Immediately
> his leprosy was cleansed. (Matthew 8:2–3)

A loud cry from the Lord Jesus Christ raised Lazarus from the dead four days after burial (John 11:43–44). A touch from the Lord Jesus Christ healed the mother-in-law of Peter (Matthew 8:14–15). The Lord did not use surgical tools to heal the sick; He used the healing power of God.

3. How did the apostles of Christ perform miracles after Jesus' resurrection and ascension to heaven?

The apostles performed these miracles in the name of and by the power of Jesus. The Apostle Peter said to the lame man outside the temple gate:

"Silver and gold I do not have, but what I do have I give you: In the name of Jesus Christ of Nazareth, rise up and walk." And he took him by the right hand and lifted him up, and immediately his feet and ankle bones received strength. So he, leaping up, stood and walked and entered the temple with them—walking, leaping, and praising God. (Acts 3:6–8)

In addition, when Peter went to visit the saints in Lydda, he healed the paralyzed man by the power of Jesus Christ:

And Peter said to him, "Aeneas, Jesus the Christ heals you. Arise and make your bed." Then he arose immediately. (Acts 9:34)

We see a similar thing when the Apostle Paul met the sorcerer/fake Jewish prophet who wanted to prevent the deputy, Sergius, from believing the Word of God:

And [Paul] said, "O full of all deceit and all fraud, you son of the devil, you enemy of all righteousness, will you not cease perverting the straight ways of the Lord? And now, indeed, the hand of the Lord is upon you, and you shall be blind, not seeing the sun for a time."

And immediately a dark mist fell on him, and he went around seeking someone to lead him by the hand. Then the proconsul believed, when he saw what had been done, being astonished at the teaching of the Lord. (Acts 13:10–12)

These miracles were done only in the name, authority, and power of Jesus Christ, the Lord.

4. In whose name does Mary make her miracles?

We do not hear anything about the name of the Lord Jesus amidst the rumors of miracles done by Mary. Have you ever questioned that? God Almighty has given us minds with which to think and to differentiate through the light of His Word. He has inspired His prophets and apostles, enabling them to differentiate between what is right and what is wrong and between darkness and light. We need to know that ignorance, the unenlightened mind, is a fertile ground for sin:

> For from within, out of the heart of men, proceed
> evil thoughts, adulteries, fornications, murders,
> thefts, covetousness, wickedness, deceit, lewd-
> ness, an evil eye, blasphemy, pride, foolishness.
> (Mark 7:21–22)

It is a dangerous thing to passively depend on human knowledge and choose to remain ignorant of God's truth in His Word. Let us go back to the Scriptures that are clear and pure from every deception like those contained

in human earthly traditions. We would like to assure you
that none of the New Testament books ever recorded even
one miracle that blessed Mary had performed in her lifetime; and she certainly had no power to perform miracles
after her death.

Our Lord's mother does not have the qualities of deity;
she is not omnipotent (having the power to do everything),
she is not omniscient (knowing everything), and she is not
omnipresent (able to be present everywhere at once). Only
the Triune God has these attributes.

Let us remember the kings who came from the East
and heard from the prophecy that Jesus was to be born in
Bethlehem (Micah 5:2). They had seen His star in the East
and had come to Bethlehem with the goal of worshipping
that newborn King. The star preceded them and led them
until it stopped over the place where the child was born:

> And when they had come into the house, they
> saw the young Child with Mary His mother,
> and fell down and worshiped Him. And when
> they had opened their treasures, they presented
> gifts to Him: gold, frankincense, and myrrh.
> (Matthew 2:11)

The kings kneeled to Jesus, they did not kneel to Mary
His mother; they presented gifts to Jesus, not to Mary.
The kneeling, the honor, and the gifts were all given to

Jesus. These wise men (kings) did this even in the presence of Mary who was standing there in the midst of that wonderful scene.

It is appropriate to mention Peter's response when Cornelius the Centurion fell down at Peter's feet and worshipped him. Peter did not accept homage from Cornelius:

> But Peter lifted him up, saying, "Stand up;
> I myself am also a man." (Acts 10:26)

We believe that if blessed Mary were to come back to life and see the pictures of herself hanging in the churches, some painted with her carrying the baby Jesus and showing a halo of light over her head (much larger than the halo over His); if Mary were to hear the prayers being raised by those believing in her miracles, see the priests offering incense to icons picturing her, and see her statues being sold to Christians to glorify her—she would be shocked. She would say to those glorifying her and giving her credit for miracles, a similar thing that Peter told Cornelius, "Stop praying to me. Stop having faith in my power. I am a servant and handmaiden of the Lord, not a goddess, I, myself, am also a woman."

Let blessed Mary be in her rightly honored place, where the Bible has put her:

- Blessed among women,

- To be blessed by all generations,

- An example of purity and sanctification,

- A role model for having faith in the ability and power of her God—the Almighty God,

- The woman who believed all that was said to her even though it was beyond the natural,

- The woman who continued praying *to the Lord* with the disciples and the other women followers of Christ (they were not praying *to her*),

- The woman God made to be the vessel of honor through whom the Son of God would be born, and

- The woman about whom the Holy Spirit intended the last thing to be written in the New Testament was that she was among the brethren, waiting in prayer in obedience to the words of Christ (Acts 1:14).

CONCLUSION

*T*HE earthly mother of our Savior, Jesus Christ, is a worthy example for all Christians for her faith in God and her obedience to do His will even in the most difficult circumstances. She was also obedient to the Son of her earthly womb. She progressively came to recognize Him as her Creator—God in the flesh:

> All things were created through Him and for Him. (Colossians 1:16)

Therefore, as she tells the servants at the wedding in Cana, *"Whatever He says to you, do it"* (John 2:5), this is also the honorable Mary's valuable advice for us to follow today. To follow her advice means that we accept Jesus' words, "I am the way, the truth, and the life. No one comes to the Father except through Me" (John 14:6).

In addition, Christ commands us to repent so that we can join Him as faithful servants in the Kingdom of God. One of His last commands was to go into the entire world and make more disciples for Him. Our prayer is that all of us who claim to have followed Him in His first command by turning to God from self and sin will obey Christ's second command to join Him in being concerned for others who do not yet know Him.

Informal Lexicon of Leading Ideas

(Common religious terms re Mary and the Gospel in typical use in the traditional churches)[1]

Compiled by Ronald W. Kirk, Theology Editor

Ordered by Concepts

Mary

Veneration (of Mary) (Introduction)
Mary, Mother of Jesus (Ch. 1)
Virgin (Ch. 1)
Miracle (Ch. 6)
Mediator (Ch. 7)
Bodily Assumption or Ascension (Ch. 8)
Appearance, or Apparition of
    Mary (Ch. 11)
Immaculate Conception

The Gospel

Bible, Word of God (Introduction)
Holy (Introduction)
Faith (Ch. 1)
(God the Holy) Trinity (Ch. 1)
Heavenly Father (Ch. 3)
Jesus Christ, Prince of Peace (Intro.)
Holy Ghost, Holy Spirit (Ch. 1)
Gospel (Ch. 3)
Grace (Ch. 1)
Angel (Introduction)
Priest (Ch. 1)
Saint (Ch. 6)
Worship (Ch. 9)
Demon (Ch. 11)
False God, Idol
Communion

Alphabetical List

Angel
Appearance or Apparition of Mary
Assumption or Ascension (Bodily)
Bodily Assumption or Ascension
Bible, Word of God, Scriptures
Communion
Demon
Faith
False God, Idol
God the Holy Trinity
Gospel
Grace
Heavenly Father
Holy
Holy Ghost, Holy Spirit
Idol, False God
Immaculate Conception
Jesus Christ, Prince of Peace
Mary, Mother of Jesus
Mediator
Miracle
Priest
Saint
Veneration (of Mary)
Virgin
Worship

---

1 Except as noted, definitions are excerpted from Noah Webster, *An American Dictionary of the English Language* (Facsimile 1828 Edition). Chesapeake, VA: Foundation for American Christian Education (FACE), 1967, 1995; also available on CD.

129

Mary

Veneration (and Honor of Mary) (Introduction)

The highest degree of respect and reverence; respect mingled with some degree of awe; a feeling or sentiment excited by the dignity and superiority of a person, or by the sacredness of his character, and with regard to place, by its consecration to sacred services.

We find a secret awe and veneration for one who moves above us in a regular and illustrious course of virtue. –Addison.

[EDITOR'S NOTE: All Biblical Christians venerate her (Luke 1:8). By definition, venerating Mary is giving her due honor. The difficulty arises when people elevate Mary to a status equal to or greater than that of Christ, either through worship in the heart, in prayer, or in religious practice.]

Mary, Mother of Jesus (Chapter 1)

[EDITOR'S NOTE: The virgin young woman, betrothed to Joseph, who gave birth to Jesus (Luke 1:26-38; Matthew 1:16-25).]

Virgin (Chapter 1)

a. Pure, untouched, chaste.

n. A woman who has had no carnal knowledge of man.

[EDITOR'S NOTE: Mary was a virgin—that is, she had no sexual relations, prior to the birth of Jesus.]

Miracle (Chapter 6)

1. Literally, a wonder or wonderful thing; but appropriately,
2. In *theology*, an event or effect contrary to the established constitution and course of things, or a deviation from the known laws of nature; a supernatural event. *Miracles* can be wrought only by Almighty power, as when Christ healed lepers, saying, "I will, be thou clean," or calmed the tempest, "Peace, be still."

   They considered not the miracle *of the loaves.* Mark 6.

   A man approved of God by miracles *and signs.* Acts 2.

Mediator (Chapter 7)

1. One that interposes between parties at variance for the purpose of reconciling them.
2. By way of eminence, Christ is THE MEDIATOR, the divine intercessor through whom sinners may be reconciled to an offended God. Tim. 2.

Christ is a mediator *by nature, as partaking of both natures divine and human; and* mediator *by office, as transacting matters between God and man.* –Waterland.

Bodily Assumption or Ascension (Chapter 8)

Ascension The act of ascending; a rising, as of our Savior to Heaven.

Assumption In the Romish Church, the taking up of a person into heaven, as the virgin Mary, and festival honoring that event.

From CatholicAnswers[2]

> "The doctrine of the Assumption says that at the end of her life on earth Mary was assumed, body and soul, into heaven, just as Enoch, Elijah, and perhaps others had been before her. It's also necessary to keep in mind what the Assumption is not. Some people think Catholics believe Mary 'ascended' into heaven. That's not correct. Christ, by his own power, ascended into heaven. Mary was assumed or taken up into heaven by God. She didn't do it under her own power."

[EDITOR'S NOTE: Assumption is passive, while ascension may be taken as active. "The Church has never formally defined whether she died or not, and the integrity of the doctrine of the Assumption would not be impaired if she did not in fact die, but the almost universal consensus is that she did die. Pope Pius XII, in Munificentissimus Deus (1950), defined that Mary, 'after the completion of her earthly life' (note the silence regarding her death), 'was assumed body and soul into the glory of heaven.'"[2]]

Appearance, Apparition of Mary (Chapter 11)

Apparition

2. The thing appearing; a visible object; a form. –Milton; –Shak.

3. A ghost; a specter; a visible spirit. [This is now the usual sense of the word.]

4. Mere appearance, opposed to reality. –Denham

[EDITOR'S NOTE: The unscriptural belief in Mary's supernatural appearances is contrary to the centrality of Christ, who only is to be glorified. Such appearances may be in ordinary objects or as an apparition or spirit. As the author cites, given that ghostly human spirits do not occupy the earth, many Christians believe that these are deceptive manifestations of the evil one (2 Corinthians 11:14).]

---

2 "Immaculate Conception and Assumption," from *Catholic Answers*, one of the nation's largest lay-run apostolates of Catholic apologetics and evangelization: www.catholic.com/library/Immaculate_Conception_and_sssum.asp. Accessed Dec. 6, 2010.

Immaculate Conception

Immaculate

1. Spotless; pure; unstained; undefiled; without blemish; as *immaculate* reputation; *immaculate* thoughts. Our Savior has set us an example of an *immaculate* life and conversation.

From CatholicAnswers[3]

The Immaculate Conception (officially defined by Pope Pius IX in 1854) means that Mary, whose conception was brought about the normal way, was herself conceived without original sin or its stain—that's what "immaculate" means: without stain. The essence of original sin is the deprivation of sanctifying grace, and its stain is a corrupt nature. Many believe based on the Scripture verse "full of grace," that Mary, by God's grace, was in the state of sanctifying grace and free from the corrupt nature original sin brings.

[EDITOR'S NOTE: Immaculate conception is a doctrine found in the Roman Catholic Church and is denied emphatically by almost all other churches.]

The Gospel

The Bible (the Word of God, Scriptures) (Introduction)

THE BOOK, by way of eminence; the sacred volume, in which are contained the revelations of God, the principles of Christian faith, and the rules of practice. It consists of two parts, called the Old and New Testaments.

The Bible *should be the standard of language as well as of faith.* –Anon.

[EDITOR'S NOTE: The Bible, properly speaking, is a collection or library of books. The Bible is the very Word of God to man, through inspiration of men by the Holy Spirit. The ground upon which Christians accept the books of the Bible as God's Word is the very nature of God Himself as revealed in those Scriptures. That is, the good and loving God reveals Himself to men for our redemption and abundant life. The Bible is self-affirming truth, proving itself to be a supernatural message from beyond time by writing history before it happened. God further assures us of the Bible's trustworthy veracity because it proves to be true in real life. Upon our accepting the Bible as God's Word, all experience affirms the Bible as the Word of God! Upon

---

3 "Immaculate Conception and Assumption," from *Catholic Answers* Website.

submitting to God's requirement that we trust in Him and walk by faith, everything else follows.]

Holy (Introduction)

Whole, entire, complete, sound, unimpaired.

1. Properly, whole, entire, or perfect, in a moral sense. Hence, pure in heart, temper or dispositions; free from sin and sinful affections. Applied to the Supreme Being, *holy* signifies perfectly pure, immaculate, and complete in moral character; and man is more or less *holy*, as his heart is more or less sanctified, or purified from evil dispositions. We call a man *holy*, when his heart is conformed in some degree to the image of God, and his life is regulated by the divine precepts. Hence, *holy* is used as nearly synonymous with good, pious, godly.

    Be ye holy; *for I am* holy. 1 Pet. 1.

2. Hallowed; consecrated, or set apart to a sacred use, or to the service or worship of God; a sense frequent in Scripture; as the *holy* sabbath; *holy* oil; *holy* vessels; a *holy* nation; the *holy* temple; a *holy* priesthood.

3. Proceeding from pious principles, or directed to pious purposes; as *holy* zeal.

4. Perfectly just and good; as the *holy* law of God.

5. Sacred; as a *holy* witness.

[EDITOR'S NOTE: The Hebrew word for *holy* essentially means *clean*.[4] In Greek, the term is *hagios* from the root *hagos*, an awful thing. This is the original sense of awful—full of awe. It means the fear that recognition of God inspires. God is Holy. Other words in both the Old and New Testaments, such as *saint, sacred,* or *hallowed*, mean essentially the same thing. Typically, Bible expositors render the term *holy* to be separated unto God, but that understanding is unduly limited. Holiness is much more than positional, and expresses an internal quality. Consider the Hebrew term for *holy* meaning clean. When something is unclean, it is impure. Even small impurities destroy essential good qualities. So we say, a fly in the ointment, or

---

4 For example, "qadash, kaw-dash'; a prim. root; *to be* (causat. make, pronounce or observe as) *clean* (ceremonially or morally):-appoint, bid, consecrate, dedicate, defile, hallow, (be, keep) *holy* (-er, place), keep, prepare, proclaim, purify, sanctify (-ied one, self), X *wholly*." (Hebrew and Chaldee Dictionary, James Strong, *Strong's Exhaustive Concordance of the Bible*. Nashville: Thomas Nelson Inc., Publishers, 1979, entry 6942).

one bad apple spoils the whole barrel. The Bible says a little leaven leavens the whole lump. God, including His Son, is absolutely pure, absolutely good. God's people are *holy* because God through Christ makes us so. Otherwise, we are sinful, impure, polluted. Thus, for men Christian holiness is had entirely by faith.]

Faith (Chapter 1)

1. Belief; the assent of the mind to the truth of what is declared by another, resting on his authority and veracity, without other evidence; the judgment that what another states or testifies is the truth. I have strong *faith* or no *faith* in the testimony of a witness, or in what a historian narrates.

2. The assent of the mind to the truth of a proposition advanced by another; belief, on probable evidence of any kind.

3. In *theology*, the assent of the mind or understanding to the truth of what God has revealed. Simple belief of the Scriptures, of the being and perfections of God, and of the existence, character, and doctrines of Christ, founded on the testimony of the sacred writers, is called *historical or speculative faith.*

4. Evangelical, justifying, or saving *faith*, is the assent of the mind to the truth of divine revelation, on the authority of God's testimony, accompanied with a cordial assent of the will or approbation of the heart; an entire confidence or trust in God's character and declarations, and in the character and doctrines of Christ, with an unreserved surrender of the will to his guidance, and dependence on his merits for salvation. In other words, that firm belief of God's testimony, and of the truth of the gospel, which influences the will, and leads to an entire reliance on Christ for salvation.

   Being justified by faith. Rom. 5.

   Without faith *it is impossible to please God.* Heb. 11.

   For we walk by faith, *not by sight.* 2 Cor. 2:5.

   With the heart man believeth to righteousness. Rom. 10.

   The faith *of the gospel is that emotion of the mind, which is called trust or confidence, exercised toward the moral character of God, and particularly of the Savior.* –Dwight

   Faith *is an affectionate practical confidence in the testimony of God.* –J. Hawes

   Faith *is a firm, cordial belief in the veracity of God, in all the*

*declarations of his word; or a full and affectionate confidence
in the certainty of those things which God has declared,
and because he has declared them.* −L. Woods

5. The object of belief; a doctrine or system of doctrines believed;
a system of revealed truths received by [C]hristians.

*They heard only, that he who persecuted us in times past,
now preacheth the faith which once he destroyed.* −Gal. 1

6. The promises of God, or [H]is truth and faithfulness.

*Shall their unbelief make the faith of God without
effect?* Rom. 3

7. An open profession of gospel truth.

Your faith is spoken of throughout the whole world. Rom. 1

[EDITOR's NOTE: Biblical faith requires men to trust God against their
own better—albeit sinful—judgment. God requires faith as a basis
of restored relationship with Him. Faith counters the original sin of
man seeking to make himself equal, in his understanding of things,
with God.]

(God the Holy) Trinity (Chapter 1)

Trinity Three and unity or one.

In *theology*, the union of three persons in one Godhead, the Father,
the Son, and the Holy Spirit.

*In my whole essay, there is not any thing like an objection
against the Trinity.* −Locke.

[EDITOR's NOTE: Following are three common terms for the persons
of the Holy Trinity—Father, Son, and Holy Spirit.]

Heavenly Father (Chapter 3)

Father [see also God, p. 137]

1. He who begets a child; in L. *genitor* or *generator*.

The father *of a fool hath no joy.* Prov. 17.

A wise son maketh a glad father. Prov. 10.

9. The appellation of the first person in the adorable Trinity.

*Go ye, therefore, and teach all nations, baptizing them in the name
of the* Father, *and of the Son, and of the Holy Spirit.* Matt. 28.

[EDITOR's NOTE: The term Heavenly Father distinguishes the Father
God from earthly and mortal fathers, while capturing the sense of
God as personal and loving like an earthly father, but with no flaws
or limits to His goodness toward us.]

Jesus Christ, Son of God, Prince of Peace (Introduction)

Christ: The ANOINTED; an appellation given to the Savior of the world, and synonymous with the Hebrew MESSIAH. It was a custom of antiquity to consecrate persons to the sacerdotal and regal offices by anointing them with oil.

Prince: In *Scripture*, this name *prince* is given to God, Dan. 8; to Christ, who is called the *prince* of peace, Is. 9.

[EDITOR'S NOTE: Christ the *Son* is the second person of the Holy Trinity (Matthew 3:17, 14:33). It is Christ alone through Whom we have peace with God, and ultimately with each other (Luke 2:14; John 14:27).]

Holy Ghost, Holy Spirit (Chapter 1)

The *Holy Ghost* is the third person in the adorable Trinity. *Scripture*. *Holy Spirit*, the third person in the Trinity.

[EDITOR'S NOTE: The terms Holy Ghost and Holy spirit are synonymous. The terms arise from the difference between seventeenth century usage and contemporary usage, as is often the case, since English is historically a composite of several contributing languages.]

Gospel (Chapter 3)

A good or joyful message.

1. The history of the birth, life, actions, death, resurrection, ascension, and doctrines of Jesus Christ; or a revelation of the grace of God to fallen man through a mediator, including the character, actions, and doctrines of Christ, with the whole scheme of salvation, as revealed by Christ and [H]is apostles. This *gospel* is said to have been preached to Abraham, by the promise *"in thee shall all nations be blessed."* Gal. 3:8.

    It is called the gospel *of God*. Rom. 1:1.
    It is called the gospel *of Christ*. Rom. 1:16.
    It is called the gospel *of salvation*. Eph. 1:13.

2. *God's word.* –Hammond.
3. *Divinity; theology.* –Milton.

[EDITOR'S NOTE: The Biblical word Gospel essentially means good news. The good news is the message of Christ in all its significance, especially salvation through God's grace, by faith (e.g., Matthew 4:23).]

Grace (Chapter 1)

1. Favor; good will; kindness; disposition to oblige another; as a grant made as an act of *grace*.

2. Appropriately, the free unmerited love and favor of God, the spring and source of all the benefits men receive from [H]im.
   And if by grace, *then it is no more of works.* Rom. 11.
3. Favorable influence of God; divine influence or the influence of the spirit, in renewing the heart and restraining from sin.
   My grace *is sufficient for thee.* 2 Cor. 12.
4. The application of Christ's righteousness to the sinner.
   Where sin abounded, grace *did much more abound.* Rom. 5.
5. A state of reconciliation to God. Rom. 5:2.
6. Virtuous or religious affection or disposition, as a liberal disposition, faith, meekness, humility, patience, &c. proceeding from divine influence.
7. Spiritual instruction, improvement, and edification. Eph. 4:29.
8. Apostleship, or the qualifications of an apostle. Eph. 3:8.
9. Eternal life; final salvation. 1 Pet. 1:13.

[EDITOR'S NOTE: Grace is God's unmerited favor toward men of faith in Him. It is unmerited because of our inherited and innate sinfulness and rebellion against God, and evil toward men. He favors us through adoption and through provision of life and salvation through Christ.]

Angel (Introduction)

1. Literally, a messenger; one employed to communicate news or information from one person to another at a distance. But appropriately,
2. A spirit, or a spiritual intelligent being employed by God to communicate [H]is will to man. Hence *angels* are ministers of God, and ministering spirits. Heb. 1.

[EDITOR'S NOTE: The Bible says that the angels are temporarily elevated above men (Psalm 8:5; Hebrews 2:7-9; 1 Corinthians 6:3). Two angels are named in the Scriptures, Michael and Gabriel. Many believe that Michael's appearance to Daniel is a Theophany, an appearance of Christ before His incarnation. Likewise Michael is portrayed leading the angels in Revelation after the ascension (Daniel 10:13,21, 12:1; Jude 9; Revelation 12:7). The angel Gabriel also spoke to Daniel and announced to Mary the coming of Jesus (Daniel 8:15, 9:21; Luke 1:19,26).]

Priest (Chapter 1)

A man who officiates in sacred offices. Among pagans, priests were persons whose appropriate business was to offer sacrifices and perform other sacred rites of religion. In primitive ages, the fathers of families, princes and kings were priests. Thus Cain and Abel, Noah, Abraham, Melchizedeck, Job, Isaac and Jacob offered their own sacrifices. In the days of Moses, the office of priest was restricted to the tribe of Levi, and the priesthood consisted of three orders, the high priest, the priests, and the Levites, and the office was made hereditary in the family of Aaron.

Every priest *taken from among men is ordained for men in things pertaining to God, that he may offer both gifts and sacrifices for sins.* Heb. 5.

[EDITOR'S NOTE: In Hebrew, priest (*cohen*) is a mediator or go-between. In the Old Testament, the appointed priest spoke for God to men; and represented men to God. God's holiness meant that sinful man must have limited access to Him. Thus, the priests exquisitely prepared themselves according to instructions given by God, and went before Him under precise conditions. God sovereignly tore down the curtain of separation at Christ's death on the cross (Matthew 27:51). Now Christ is the sole mediator between God and man, and remains our high priest, far surpassing the agency of earthly priests (see the New Testament Book of Hebrews).]

Saint (Chapter 6)

1. A person sanctified; a holy or godly person; one eminent for piety and virtue. It is particularly applied to the apostles and other holy persons mentioned in Scripture. A hypocrite may imitate a *saint*. Ps. 16. –Addison.
2. One of the blessed in heaven. Rev. 18.
3. The holy angels are called *saints*, Deut. 33, Jude 14.
4. One canonized by the church of Rome.

[EDITOR'S NOTE: In Biblical terms, saints, often referred to as many thousands, are all those who fear, love, praise, and walk with God. (See Deut. 33:2-3; Ps. 31:23; 1 Cor. 1:2; Eph. 2:19, 4:12.)]

Worship (Chapter 9)

[Sax. *weorthscype*; worth and ship; the state of worth or worthiness.] To adore; to pay divine honors to; to reverence with supreme respect and veneration.

Thou shalt worship *no other God.* Ex. 24
1. To perform acts of adoration
2. To perform religious service.

Our fathers worshipped *in this mountain.* Jo. 4

4. Chiefly and eminently, the act of paying divine honors to the Supreme Being; or the reverence and homage paid to [H]im in religious exercises, consisting in adoration, confession, prayer, thanksgiving and the like.

The worship of God is an eminent part of religion. —Tillotson.

Prayer is a chief part of religious worship. —Ibm.

5. Homage paid to idols or false gods by pagans; as the *worship* of Isis.

[EDITOR'S NOTE: In both the Hebrew and Greek portions of the Bible, the words translated *worship* are almost without exception bowing down in fawning submission. For proud, sinful men, worship of God is indeed a significant thing. "True worshipers will worship the Father in spirit and truth: for the Father is seeking such to worship Him" (Jo. 4:23). Worship of Mary is wrong.]

Demon (Chapter 11)

A spirit, or immaterial being, holding a middle place between men and the celestial deities of the Pagans.... The demons of the New Testament were supposed to be spiritual beings which vexed and tormented men. And in general, the word, in modern use, signifies an evil spirit or genius, which influences the conduct or directs the fortunes of mankind.

[EDITOR'S NOTE: In common usage, the term angel refers to those spiritual beings described by the Bible who continue to serve God (e.g. Luke 2:8-15), while demon refers to similar but evil creatures who joined and serve Satan (e.g. Matthew 4:24).]

False God, Idol

God

1. The Supreme Being; Jehovah; the eternal and infinite spirit, the creator, and the sovereign of the universe.

God is a spirit; and they that worship *him, must* worship *him in spirit and in truth.* John 4:24.

2. A false god; a heathen deity; an idol.

Fear not the gods of the Amorites. Judges 6.

Idol

An image, form or representation, usually of a man or other animal, consecrated as an object of worship; a pagan deity. Idols are usually statues or images, carved out of wood or stone, or formed of metals, particularly silver or gold.

The gods of the nations are idols. Ps. 96.

4. Anything on which we set our affections; that to which we indulge an excessive and sinful attachment.

Little children, keep yourselves from idols. 1 Jo. 5

An *idol* is any thing which usurps the place of God in the hearts of his rational creatures. –S. Miller

[EDITOR's NOTE: Such idols are truly manmade. God rightly accuses men of their foolishness and wickedness who worship objects made with their own hands, which can neither see nor hear, being completely inert (e.g. Is. 2:8-18). However, men have attributed power associated with such idols. Paul the Apostle addresses this when he says that though the idols may be associated with demons they yet are nothing (Romans 8:1-6). Furthermore, contemporary theology identifies anything that usurps the place of God, such as various lusts, as an idol. For our own good, God requires that He Himself be the center of our focus, obedience, and adoration.]

Communion

Fellowship; intercourse between two persons or more; interchange of transactions, or offices; a state of giving and receiving; agreement; concord.

We are naturally led to seek communion *and fellowship*
with others. –Hooker.

What communion *hath light with darkness?* 2 Cor. 6.

The communion *of the Holy Spirit be with you all.* 2 Cor. 13.

2. Mutual intercourse or union in religious worship, or in doctrine and discipline.

The Protestant churches have no *communion*
with the Romish [Roman Catholic] church.

3. The body of [C]hristians who have one common faith and discipline. The three grand *communions* into which the [C]hristian church is divided, are those of the Greek, the Romish, and the Protestant churches.

4. The act of communicating the sacrament of the eucharist; the celebration of the Lord's supper; the participation of the blessed sacrament. The fourth council of Lateran decrees that every believer shall receive the *communion* at least at Easter. –Encyc.

5. Union of professing [C]hristians in a particular church; as, members in full *communion*.

[EDITOR's NOTE: In contemporary usage, *communion* is definition four, the Lord's Table, assigned by Christ as a remembrance of Himself, and His work on our behalf (Luke 22:19-20).]

BIBLIOGRAPHY

Calvin, John. *Commentary on a Harmony of the Evangelists, Matthew, Mark, and Luke*, Volume I. (Grand Rapids: Baker Book House, 1996), 184.

El Ajbiah — the Arabic language prayer book of the Coptic Orthodox Church, printed in Cairo, Egypt.

ElMasry, Iris H. *Introduction to the Coptic Church*. (Cairo, Egypt: Dar El Alam El Arabi, 1977), 47–49. The article in the book is entitled "The Blessed Virgin." In it, the virgin Mary is called the Queen, Mother of God, Mother of the Light, Mother of the Mercy, Mother of the Grace, Ship of Safety, that she is the first and last of the saints who are to be called upon to intercede for the petitioner, she is an authoritative Mediator, that she is a perpetual virgin and those who are called Jesus' brothers and sisters in the gospels were really his cousins, that Mary takes precedence over the celestial hosts, and that her body after death was not left in the earth to decay but was carried to heaven by the angels. The Coptic Church celebrates this Day of Assumption every August 22.

Lange, John Peter. *Commentary on the Holy Scriptures, Critical, Doctrinal, and Homiletical*. (Grand Rapids: Zondervan Publishing House, 1960), Volume 12, 9–12.

Neander, Augustus. *General History of the Christian Religion and Church*, Volumes I & III. (London: Henry G. Bohn, 1851). Volume I possesses an excellent treatment of the factions, persecutions, and character of the church in the early era of the church, in "Section First, Relation of the Christian Church to the unchristian World," 95–247.

Noll, Most Rev. John Francis D.D, LL.D. and Rev. Lester J. Fallon, C.M., S.T.D. *Father Smith Instructs Jackson.* (Huntington, Indiana: Our Sunday Visitor Press, 1960). On page 21, this book gives the Roman Catholic teaching that the virgin Mary was preserved from original sin from the time she was conceived. Pages 51–54, entitled "'The Bible Only' Theory Has Proved a Failure," refer to the Roman Catholic Church's teaching on the danger for the laity to attempt to interpret Scripture without the Catholic Church's interpretation. On page 206, in the teaching about "The Hail Mary, Mother of God" prayer, the authors say that just as we greet our heavenly Father in the Lord's Prayer and ask for His help, we greet our heavenly Mother and ask her to offer her powerful prayers on our behalf. On page 210, in the teaching on the Rosary, the authors say that the Rosary includes meditation on the mysteries in the "Blessed Mother's life such as the Assumption of Mary into Heaven and her Coronation in Heaven." Page 211 says that both God and Christ's Blessed Mother hear and reward prayers.

Shakir, M. H., Editor. *The Qur'an Translation, 13th U.S. Edition.* (Elmhurst, NY: Tahrike Tarsile Qur'an Inc.: 2002).

Shenuda, Pope, of Alexandria, Egypt. Articles in *Mar Yohana*, Coptic Orthodox magazine. (Covina, CA: 2005).

Vine, W. E., Merrill F. Unger, William White, Jr. *Vine's*

BIBLIOGRAPHY

Complete Expository Dictionary of Old and New Testament Words. (Nashville: Thomas Nelson Publishers, 1996).

Walker, Williston. *A History of the Christian Church,* Third Edition. (NY: Charles Scribner's Sons, 1970), 125.

Webster's New Collegiate Dictionary, 6th Edition. (Merriam-Webster Publishing Company).

Mary, Did You Know?

Mary, did you know that your baby boy
would someday walk on water?
Mary, did you know that your baby boy
would save our sons and daughters?
Did you know that your baby boy
has come to make you new?
This Child that you delivered
will soon deliver you.

Mary, did you know that your baby boy
will give sight to the blind man?
Mary, did you know that your baby boy
would calm a storm with His hand?
Did you know that your baby boy
has walked where angels trod?
And when you kiss your little baby,
you've kissed the face of God?
Mary, did you know...?

The blind will see, the deaf will hear;
the dead will live a-gain!
The lame will leap, the dumb will speak
the praises of the Lamb!
Mary, did you know that your baby boy
is Lord of all creation?
Mary, did you know that your baby boy
will one day rule the nations?
Did you know that your baby boy
is heaven's perfect Lamb?
And the sleeping Child you're holding
is the Great I AM!

Written by Mark Lowry and Buddy Greene
Performed by Michael English
© 1991, 1993 Word Music, LLC (a div. of Word, Inc)/Refus Music
(admin by Gaither Copyright Management).
All rights reserved. Used by permission.

DR.
LABIB
MIKHAIL

AUTHOR

*D*R. MIKHAIL, born in Egypt on July 23, 1920, is a journalist, counselor, and television and radio speaker. He is the author of more than eighty books in Arabic, English, and Spanish. He writes on the most important issues of our times and God uses his books to bring many people to the kingdom of Jesus Christ. His books are well received all over the world, and several of them are in the third or fifth printing.

Dr. Mikhail holds earned degrees including B.A., M.A., and Th.D. from the International Bible Institute and Seminary. The author is well acquainted and experienced in the teachings and practices of the traditional churches. He has studied extensively the writings and theology of the famous Egyptian theologian of the Scriptures, the fourth century Saint Athanasius of Alexandria, who helped to clarify the early doctrines of the Christian Church.

He was the President of the General Bible Baptist Council in Egypt for five years. He was professor of Homiletics, Psychology, and Church History at Faith Mission Bible College in Cairo, Egypt, for three years.

He has preached to thousands in evangelistic campaigns throughout the major cities of Egypt and Lebanon, and also in Baghdad, Iraq; London, England; and Germany. He has lectured in many seminars and conferences in the United States of America, Canada, and in Jerusalem, Israel.

Prior to moving to the United States in 1973, Dr. Mikhail founded and pastored churches in Egypt for thirty-four years. Dr. Mikhail pastored Evangelical Bible Church in Fairfax, Virginia, for ten years. He retired in December 1992 to consecrate his time to writing.

He wrote this book to help the believers to deepen their relationship with Jesus Christ, and experience peace, joy, and a victorious life when they come to the point of saying wholeheartedly, "I Surrender All."

DR. NASSER S. FARAG

TRANSLATOR AND
CONTRIBUTOR TO
THE SPANISH AND
ENGLISH EDITIONS

*D*R. FARAG is the son of a pioneer Anderson, Indiana, Church of God (COG) family in Egypt. His father published Christian books, magazines, and hymnals. He studied teaching, social work, and counseling from 1955–1966 in Egypt and Holland. From 1963–69, he served with the Near East Christian Council in Cairo and Gaza, and as a chaplain with the Baptist Mission Hospital in Yemen. During the 1967 conflict in Gaza, he married Marilyn Sheaffer who was directing the Baptist Mission School of Nursing there. After finishing his theological education in Anderson, Indiana, they served with the COG in Egypt, Kenya, and Mexico. In 1979, Nasser earned his D.Min. degree from Midwestern Baptist Seminary and later did post-doctoral mission studies at Asbury Theological Seminary.

Later, Dr. Farag chaired the Missions Department, taught, and directed the third world simulated village, H.E.A.R.T., missionary training program of Warner Southern University in Florida, and served in Haiti, Belize, and Mexico.

In 1996, Nasser and Marilyn started Truth in Love Ministry, a non-denominational, cross-cultural, counter-cults outreach. They do volunteer seminars on "True Power of the Holy Spirit," "Cults," "Cultural-Geographical Background of Bible Interpretation," "Islam in the Light of the Bible," "Third World Health and Nutrition," "Christian Women's Leadership," and "Ministerial Ethics." These have been conducted in the United States, six Latin American countries, fourteen African countries, and India.

Dr. Farag is the author of a non-confrontational apologetic/evangelistic book that expresses the ultimate greatness of God only in Christ, the Incarnate Word, in comparison with other prophets and so-called prophets. The book allows nothing but the light of Christ to dispense the darkness of all unscriptural teachings and practices. To the Glory of GOD, that book has been distributed in several countries in English, French, Arabic, Turkish, Spanish, Oriya, Hindi, and Swahili. The Farsi translation is underway.

THE PUBLISHER'S WORD

[T]he Virgin shall conceive and bear a Son,
and shall call His name Immanuel [God with us].
(Isaiah 7:14)

[M]y spirit has rejoiced in God my Savior.
For He has regarded the lowly state of His maidservant.
(Luke 1:47-48a)

The Holy Spirit will come upon you,
and the power of the Highest will overshadow you;
therefore, also, that Holy One who is to be born
will be called the Son of God.
(Luke 1:35)

He is also able to save to the uttermost
those who come to God through Him,
since He ever lives to make intercession for them.
(Hebrews 7:25)

*T*HE *Virgin Mary in Light of the Word of God* is an elegant and comprehensive book on what the Bible has to say about Jesus' mother Mary. Originally published in Arabic, and then Spanish, it has already received distribution in Africa, South America, and the Middle East. Even now, Dr. Nasser Farag is distributing an advance copy of the English translation to several leaders on the mission field in Africa. Nordskog Publishing is pleased to present the finished English language edition.

In *The Virgin Mary,* Dr. Labib Mikhail makes an important contribution to Christian literature as he systematically identifies the Scriptures concerning blessed Mary, the mother of Jesus, and draws Biblically sound conclusions. As you will read in the biographies, author Dr. Labib Mikhail, and his literary partner in this work, Dr. Farag, each have an amazing lifetime of accomplishment in God's Word, in living for Christ, and in educational, missionary and evangelism work in many fields of service around the world. Their depth of accomplishment and Biblical wisdom reveal themselves in the elegant style and pointed message of *The Virgin Mary.*

Dr. Labib, over the traditions of men, fervently teaches the Holy Bible as the very Word of God. In this, he provides a tremendous ministry to those who rely on tradition at the expense of Biblical truth. The tradition-imposed diminishment of power for godly living and the resulting lack of blessings can be effectively countered by this clear enlightenment from God's Word.

As the book reveals, the veneration of blessed Mary by the churches has led to the wrongful conclusion by Muslims that Mary is a person of the Holy Trinity. While this notion is clearly untrue, Mary's veneration in the traditional churches nonetheless adds weight to the erroneous conclusion that Christianity is a false religion which denies the oneness of God. Moreover, in the traditional churches themselves, dependency on Mary as an intermediary at the expense of a personal relationship with Christ has demoralized many Christians who by that choice deny themselves the power of the Word of God and the true Gospel.

For those not well acquainted with but interested in Christianity and its true historic beliefs, you will find a straightforward declaration of the Gospel of Jesus Christ that leads to salvation and the abundant life that our God always intended for mankind, through the saving and sanctifying work of Jesus Christ.

For the committed Christian, you will find an edifying presentation of the true Gospel and of sound doctrine.

The Virgin Mary in Light of the Word of God is an eminently worthwhile book for every reader. It is not burdensome. No esoteric theological language here, this book is accessible to anyone who seeks to know the truth regarding the great figure of blessed Mary, the sound reasons to honor her and emulate her faith and character, and the glorious Good News of Jesus Christ from Mary's point of view.

This book is full of truth. It glorifies God and His Son, our Savior, Jesus Christ. Please read, enjoy, and let this book minister to your heart for the glory of God and the furthering of His kingdom.

Gerald Christian Nordskog
Publisher
January 1, Year of Our Lord, 2011

153

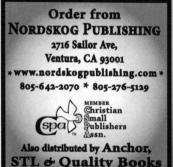

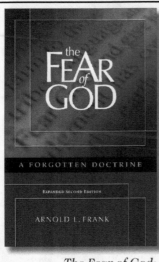

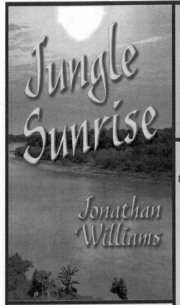